A Year at Bottengoms Farm

Other books by Ronald Blythe

A YEAR AT
BOTTENGOMS FARM

RONALD BLYTHE

CANTERBURY
PRESS

Norwich

First published in 2006 by the
Canterbury Press Norwich
(a publishing imprint of Hymns Ancient & Modern
Limited, a registered charity)
9–17 St Alban's Place, London N1 0NX

www.scm-canterburypress.co.uk

ISBN-10: 1-85311-759-5
ISBN-13: 978-1-85311-759-6

Typeset by Rowland Phototypesetting Ltd,
Bury St Edmunds, Suffolk
Printed and bound in Great Britain by
William Clowes Ltd, Beccles, Suffolk

For Gordon Brown

CONTENTS

FOREWORD

I don't know what the old Suffolk-Essex farmers and their wives would have said to such diary entries in their ancient house. The wives would have gone to church in a dogcart, the children would have walked via the hilly meadows and woods, keeping the River Stour to the right of them. It was about two miles. The bells can just about be heard on a wind in the right direction day. The farm began as a yeoman's but would end up as a tenantry. The house was made from the wood of a previous building. There still is water, water everywhere, the land being part of the water-table of the river. A mile of rough track leads down to Bottengoms which is probably Saxon.

These pages first appeared in *Church Times*.

Hauntings

January 6th

Seeing an ancient hall bedizened with Christmas lights from apex to moat, I thought how M. R. James would have disapproved. He remains our ghost-story teller extraordinary, and for him the halls and churches of East Anglia were places of shadows, of half-seen things, of inexplicable sounds, of bumps in the day as well as in the night. 'If any of my stories succeed in causing their readers to feel pleasantly uncomfortable when walking along a solitary road at nightfall, or sitting over a dying fire in the small hours, my purpose in writing them will have been attained.' He is being disingenuous. Far from making us pleasantly uncomfortable he frightens the life out of us. He was successively the Provost of Eton and King's, and a master of decay, whether of building, landscape or person. He was too, of course, the son of a Victorian country rector. In youth he was strikingly like Stephen Fry in appearance. Although an excellent cranky historian, he saw himself as an antiquary, and although the dons and collectors and parsons of his tales are presented as conventional types, they are in fact scary examples of learnèd lonely bachelors going potty. M. R. James's masterpiece is 'Oh, Whistle, and I'll Come to You, My Lad'. He died after a visit to Kew Gardens in June 1935, leaving us edgy and wintry, and with

1

a far from Pevsner view of our stained glass and flint towers.

New Year brought the ghosts out. The melancholy ever-rolling stream of Time through dark old rooms, the tilting photographs of past incumbents in damp vestries, the melting ice in dank shrubberies, the unwanted (or possibly longed for) companion catching one up in the foggy lane, and history seen as a medieval box of unholy tricks to poke about in, these were among the experiences of January. A sense not of beginnings but of endings. The churchyard filled up with winter graves. Neighbours died but did not quite depart. The novelists and writers generally, Charles Dickens, Le Fanu, had a field day. Old wives' tales came true, at least for little John Clare, humping flour from Maxey Mill and hardly daring to pass certain spots along the way. As children, we had to pass the Satan Tree, an innocent hawthorn of vast dimension which had been hung about with this libel for ages, though it was impossible to tell why. But there was a need to be frightened and it was a poor sort of village which lacked something that would put the wind up both inhabitant and traveller. Our trump card was Borley Rectory, just down the road. It had actually burnt down about the same time as M. R. James went to Paradise via Kew Gardens, but this did not exorcise its ghost, a nun, of course. My old friend James Turner and his wife occupied the coach house. I can hear him now, rattling out novels on his Remington typewriter, whilst the apple wood splintered in the grate. We were ardent Jamesians, though I was actually apostate, enjoying the horror but unbelieving, a sightseer in the haunted nest. The Turners were movers but they never took a house without a ghost. Nor at that time did it ever strike us that we should not be so entertained by the supernatural darkness when it was the Epiphany. There was so little light before gas and electricity, and so little could be done. No warmth except by the fireside. The flames danced and another world took shape.

Paul and the Slave Trade

January 10th

The mad axemen have departed leaving a fine view. First James the novelist from Italy and then Mark from just up the road. Such coppicing and logging had not been seen and heard at Bottengoms for years. Now I can look out for miles. Neighbours have come into focus, villages even. And the silence, now that the whining saws have died away, is something to cherish. The chainsaw men allowed me to do footling tasks, such as transplant a nice discovery of hart's-tongue fern (*Phyllitis scolopendrium*) from under a blackberry bush to the bank of the stream, to pile the 'rubbish' and to exclaim at their prowess. Mark and his wife bumped up the track in their Jeep with their wooden loot. Stour-light poured in from all directions. Sawdust blinded the early primroses. Birds sailed over, crossing-off ivies and willows from their nesting list. And the sweetest imaginable January air swept in. Left alone, I built bonfires, cleared tracks and listened to the early spring. The horse-ponds were like glass, the top one stuck with half-rolled-up marsh marigolds, the lower one a long, glinting watery diamond. How strange it is to have miles of Suffolk in my sights, and for Suffolk to be able to observe once more an ancient strip of beautiful Essex. But the river itself lies low like Brer Rabbit, 'Bred en bawn in a brier-patch', as he was. Opening up a landscape always reveals further concealment. I drum this wisdom into the wild chainsaw men. Five days later one of them drives back to Lucca (in Italy) in a silver car and the other flies off to ski in Austria, leaving me with a happy ruin and unskilled tasks. The great thing in life is to know one's place.

I preach on St Paul's letter to his friend Philemon, a short note but had it been read as much as his letter to the Corinthians, say, could have prevented centuries of Christian involvement in the slave trade. Philemon – you will recollect – owned a slave named Onesimus ('Profitable') who ran away. Who had in fact run all the miles from Asia Minor to Rome itself to be with a man who had told his master that in Christ all men were brothers. The apostle returns Onesimus to Philemon with this note:

I appeal to you about my child, whose father I have become in this prison. I mean Onesimus, once so little use to you, but now useful indeed to both you and me. I am sending him back to you, and in doing so I am sending part of myself. I should have liked to keep him with me, to look after me as you would wish, here in prison for the gospel. But I would rather do nothing without your consent, so that your kindness may be a master not of compulsion, but of your own free will. For perhaps this is why you lost him for a time, that you might have him back for good, no longer as a slave, but as a dear brother. If, then, you count me your partner in the faith, welcome him as you would welcome me. And if he has done you any wrong, or is in your debt, put that down to my account. I will repay. Now brother, as a Christian, be generous with me, and relieve my anxiety; we are both in Christ.

What an upsetting letter for a Roman breakfast-table. Following Jesus is one thing, turning the world upside-down quite another. Very sensibly, centuries of Christians put it on file. Who could manage a sugar or cotton plantation – or the house, if it came to it – without Onesimus and his wife? Religion must be practical.

Listings

January 11th

Almost a week into Epiphany and my resolution to be in the study all the morning and in the garden all the afternoon is inviolate. I state it now, not to boast but to shame lesser mortals. A quarter of a chapter before lunch, a ton of oak leaves and moss wire-raked from the Long Walk before tea. No one knows who planted the twelve oaks but tree men reckon it was done just after the Napoleonic wars, maybe as part of the replenishing of the woodland when so much of it had gone to sea. And why twelve? The twelve Apostles, the twelve months of the year, the twelfth birthday of a farmer's child? You take your pick. The authorities may list the ancient house but the list of what happened in and around it since, say, 1590 is anyone's guess. Today there is a rocking quarter-moon as I collect the tools and much bird-clatter in the hazels as I stow them away. Several dogs have called on me, one or two full of rage, the others full of love. 'Days are pulling out!' says their owners. Or, 'Rather you than me!' To dwell among wits – who could ask for more?

Hugh the vet's Christmas cake for tea and Ben and his parents to share it. He is pushing eight – 'I am getting old.' We agree and shake our heads. Eight! Man that is born of woman hath but a short time to live, unlike oaks. Ben then disappears on one of his rituals, which is to read my Orlando books. I would give them to him gladly but then I would destroy the ritual, and that would never do. *Orlando the Marmalade Cat* must be secretly encountered at Bottengoms on the tall-books shelf. The old rooms have gone Puritan after Twelfth Night, with the holly and cards down. Perhaps that's it – twelve oaks for Twelfth Night. The farmhouse had celebrated more than eight birthdays when Shakespeare wrote his play, I tell Ben. The white cat, who is bad at figures, turns her gaze to the burning logs, her eyes offering gold for gold. Like W. C. Fields – 'Anybody who hates children and dogs can't be all bad' – she doesn't care for boys. But she adores hugger-mugger humanity round the hearth. Five centuries of farm cats, who can imagine it? Five hundred years of candlelight, plus a few decades of 100w bulbs. The lantern which swung through the farmyard before the last war now swings above the central heating boiler. I can remember this swinging Epiphany light when the animals were settled for the night. Sometimes I met it in a lane, its carrier invisible. We would tell each other what the weather was, windy, cold, good for ducks, and walk on. 'Is that you, John?', the light casting more shadow than illumination, so not at all like that star. Like wise men, 'Led on by light to Light we press.' It is an enchanting time, the Epiphany, this manifestation of the divine Love. Rowan Williams said that it was the clever visitors to the manger, not the ordinary folk, who endangered the Child. So-called wise men can make the worst mistakes. Long ago, when our faith was young, the Epiphany was celebrated on Jesus' baptismal day. It was then that a flood of light poured through the universe to make things plain, and all from one Star. 'All this was a long time ago', says one of T. S. Eliot's Magi, and in 'The very dead of winter' but he adds, 'I would do it again.' And I do it again and again in my fashion.

Mud Time

January 15th

Oversleeping, waking up in the – light! I don't have to grope for my watch. There it is, blazing with eight o'clock. 'Suppose you had to catch a train like Tom or Nick,' I scold myself. 'When did they last have to catch a train?' I reply. Downstairs there is mewing and wailing as the white cat rings up the RSPCA. I rush down. More light pouring through the curtains this time. The News comes on saying, 'No frost' and 'Fines for Yobs', the usual things. But eight o'clock! I put my head out of the door and stare at Little Horkesley, for it is all one can see from the front of the farmhouse. For four hundred years a Wormingford farmer has had to look at Little Horkesley. Gulls stream over the steep hillside and six horses feed along the horizon. And, as a Saki character observed, 'The grass looks as if it had been left out all night.' Oversleeping is nicely unsettling and I am unlikely to recover from it. At lunch a friend's wife whispers in my ear, 'He keeps on falling asleep at any hour of the day.' And I say, 'It is the winter – the dormouse syndrome, you know'; and she says, 'Oh.' I don't tell her that I didn't get up until 8 a.m., and that I feel as though I could walk home, it being only ten miles.

It is mud time in the village, which looks bedraggled and drab. Various damp dogs greet me and the double laurel hedge at Long's Farm heaves with starlings taking shelter from the east wind. The school is back and the playground is like a black mirror. A house is being built next to the Tudor pest-house and a digger squelches in its foundations. Life goes on after Christmas, if reluctantly. But the land itself is saying, 'Turn over and go back to sleep.' The Stour is sullen and cold, very unobliging. My face wobbles in its flow. No comfort there. 'Go home, shut the door,' it says, 'it is January.'

'It is the Epiphany,' I tell it, 'lighten up.' Enormous, invisible pike are waiting for April by the reedbeds. The Epistle reading is the touching story which Luke tells about the Lord's education – his enlightenment. Too young to understand the worry his sudden disappearance would have caused, the days slip by as he listens and asks questions in the Temple. His parents are distraught. A lively twelve-year-old all on his own in the town at Passover simply asking to be picked up. But why didn't his father and mother, knowing how bright he was, go to search for him in the Temple first?

There must be learnèd books on the education of Jesus, but I don't know of them. The brilliant storytelling comes from a tradition, but where does the intellectual teaching come from? Theologians must have supplied many an answer. As a boy I loved that 'wist' in Luke's story. It was flattering to know that Jesus spoke Old Suffolk. And Luke's last sentence is just as things should be for any young person: 'And Jesus increased in wisdom, and stature, and in favour with God and man.'

There has to come a day when a writer puts a finish to a book, and the day before I overslept was such a day. Not that such a little word would have worn me out but it would have placed a kind of hurdle across Time's path. Toying with titles, I am beginning to fancy *A Writer's Day-Book*, it being a collection of word expenditure over the years. 'What do you think?'

Lady Wisdom

January 17th

Furtive questioning on my part proves that a number of regular worshippers have no idea of the subjects in the Victorian windows – excluding that to St George and the Dragon, of course. Everyone knows about that. What did George Herbert mean when he wrote,

A man that looks on glass,
  On it may stay his eye;
Or if he pleaseth, through it pass,
  And then the heaven espy.

The poet is courteous. Enjoy the picture, if you like, but see through it to the Kingdom would be a better activity. The medieval glass would most likely have been intact in his day, the 'cleansing' coming later. I have no picture to look through as I watch a January sun pop up from behind Duncan's farmhouse like a glaring penny. With determined sloth, morning tea at the ready, I see wheeling phalanxes of black and white birds, seagulls and rooks, cross and recross the hillside, noting the horse-feed. This east window, blank though it is, serves me as a plain aid to meditation. Its glazing-bars rule what I must take in, the uncoppiced hazel, the wandering creatures, the hard line of the next parish, the weather, the occasional figure. Venturing out, the air greets me like fresh ice and the white and black birds get all mixed up. *Gloire de Dijon* roses dangle above me in sopping wet balls and the orchard glass is speared with bulbs. 'You'll catch your death!' says a voice in my head. But no, this is not how one catches death.

A letter from St Anselm's Abbey in Washington. Father Gabriel Myers has been teaching the brothers Olney hymns, it says. He has sent me a fine sermon on 'the legacy of the great English hymnwriters to Catholic spirituality', one hymn in particular is enthralling. It is William Cowper's

'Ere God has built the mountains, or raised the fruitful hills' and he links it with the Bible's wisdom literature which the Rule of Benedict recognizes as a 'down-to-earth practicality in the search for God'. Fr Gabriel and I first met at the Kilvert Society in Hereford when he was on one of those rather begrudged breaks which monks are given, and making his way from shrine to shrine, Bemerton, Clyro, Barbara Pym's Kensington, all the places made holy by wise writers. And now he is telling the Washington Benedictines all about Cowper's dog Mungo and that indispensable friend for every Christian, Lady Wisdom, whose guiding hand he sees in the perfect hymns of 'Isaac Watts, Charles Wesley, John Mason Neale and Frances Havergal'. And, as I must show him, many of those in Timothy Dudley-Smith's *A House of Praise*.

Lady Wisdom now says, 'How about breakfast?' Unwise folk make the headlines, this being their role. The white cat thunders through the flap and cries piteously for sustenance, not having been fed for over an hour. Alas, Cowper's hymn to Lady Wisdom is not in our three hymnbooks and we remain none the wiser. The editors were clearly unnerved by her, and should she by any chance appear on *Songs of Praise*, we will not be told who it was who wrote of her, for that is not the BBC's way, tunes but not authors. 'O wisest love!' wrote one of them.

The Boy who Ran

January 25th

'Not the least of this strange business', the ancient farmhouse tells me, 'is the silence. You may love it but I find it most unnatural. From Shakespeare's day to when you were a boy there never was silence here.' And behind the Gerald Finzi – 'Lo, the full, final Sacrifice' – there came the sound of bubbling coppers, rowdy poultry, rowdier boys, bawling mothers, jingling horses, singing girls, screeching pigs, recalcitrant tractors, hungry labourers, banging doors, sawings and diggings, commands and shouts. 'Now that is what I call a house,' said the house. Not this voice on the telephone saying, 'I am Gareth and our conservatory specialist is in your area.'

An old man called here some years ago and told me that it was his birthplace. He had travelled far since then, Kenya, everywhere. He climbed the steep stairs to see where he had slept with his brother and tears filled his eyes. They had swung on the beam support. His name was John Smith. 'Do you remember John Smith?' I asked Rosa. She had sung in the choir for eighty years. There was no one like her for keeping the tune. I might go out of tune in all directions, but never Rosa. Of course she knew John Smith – 'He was the boy who ran.' If we are to leave something behind, let it be our swiftness of foot.

13

Taking Matins I am startled to hear that Saul is not told by Jesus that it is hard for him 'to kick against the pricks'. This cruel goading of mules by means of a piece of wood studded with nails would upset me more than some of the atrocities of the Old Testament when I was a child and had the phrase explained to me. I saw the poor bleeding creature being forced along the dusty road. I saw the future apostle driven ever forward by Christ. It struck me as just the kind of realistic simile that he would use. But now he did not. I checked it in my Greek Testament – no kicking against the pricks. Wyclif's translation of 1 Corinthians 15 as 'Forsoth the pricke of deeth is synne.' In the King James Bible this is changed to 'The sting of death is sin.' I think we are goaded towards evil, painfully, bloodily. However, we rise to sing Canon Ellerton on the ravening wolf being stopped in his tracks by – a Shepherd, omitting verse 2, although I don't know why. Time and human conduct, nationality and custom, politeness, science, every mortal thing, have made their mark on what Jesus said all those years ago, but they have failed to distort his teaching. There is an earthy lyricism about it, a common sense and vision combined which resists language change, but who can blame some learnèd man, eager to make it accessible to ploughboys and dairy girls, the former driving oxen up and down the field, for adding a relevant sentence or two?

> *Lord, teach they Church the lesson,*
> *still in her darkest hour*
> *of weakness and of danger*
> *to trust thy hidden power.*

Returning to the conversation I am having with the farm-house, it reminds me that it never was what round here was known as a 'Tye', some remote pasture or common, Cuckoo Tye, Nedging Tye, Bulmer Tye, Kersey Tye – though some of these have grown up into villages proper – but it was a farm from the word go.

Owl Cries

January 29th

I an arrives. We are to drive to Long Melford to meet Sir John Tenniel's Ugly Duchess, aka Elizabeth Talbot, as she kneels with her grand relations in that fascinating parade of East Anglia aristocrats in the north aisle windows. Except that compared to the real inspiration for the Duchess in *Alice through the Looking-Glass* this one isn't ugly at all, just plain and dumpy. The artist had in mind a German lady. I stroll around the vast cold church thinking of Eamon Duffy's masterpiece *The Stripping of the Altars* in which the Reformation inventory of its treasures is used to reveal what was lost, what may have been gained. Saturday ramblers clump around. Welcomers at the west end maintain a kind of Greek chorus in Suffolk dialect, a continuation of local speech which must have gone on since all this portraiture in stained glass went up in the 1480s. When we go outside to visit the grave of the poet Edmund Blunden the wind takes a short cut right through us. Down below, at the far corner of the enormous green, vaguely seen like a pencil sketch, stands the pretty house which Siegfried Sassoon bought him. The pair of them used to bike around here after World War One, Blunden eager and swift like a small bird, Sassoon tall and a bit lost. Next Ian and I wander off to what remains of Borley Rectory to nod to the ghost, and then on to our friend Richard Bawden's exquisite continuation of church window figures at Belchamp St Paul's, engraved now, not painted. Fine fishes swim through St Andrew's legs. Ian studies and writes, I stare over the churchyard gate at the massive hall where Arthur Golding lived, translator extraordinary to the Reformation and the scholar-poet whose Ovid Shakespeare used in *The Tempest*. The weather is raw, unclear, and a rose-coloured fog rises from the winter corn. We climb into the snug womb of the car and wind our way to the Bell at Clare which is full of animated bundles – weekenders zipped in shapeless warmth.

Back at Bottengoms, Ian gone, I write an Epiphany sermon on St Paul's variety of gifts, choose hymns by Heber and Monsell, feed the white cat after her damp and amorous attentions, and we both settle down to a learned evening.

Various sufferers ring up to tell me about their colds and I commiserate – what else? This word comes from the Latin *miserari* – miser, wretched. Wail, wail. Don't come to church tomorrow, you will give it to the rest of us. Have you tried hot toddy? How helpful I am, better than any doctor.

During the night I listen to owls. They are such a familiar sound that I have to apply my ears to it especially. There now, hark, it is the owl, possibly the very one which dwells along the farmtrack and goes off like a bomb when I take a walk in the dark. Owl voices in flight are melancholy to us but not to them, of course. Byron thought there was only one thing sadder than owl songs. It was the phrase, 'I told you so.' John Clare was indignant with Shakespeare for calling it 'a merry note'. Merry? When did he last listen to an owl? Had he forgotten that he had once described – in *Macbeth* – an owl as 'the fatal bellman'? Which of them is hooting at this moment? Tawny owl, barn owl or little owl? The sound creates an unbridgeable gulf between humanity and bird, between time and eternity. But in his *Sweet Suffolk Owl* a Tudor musician says, 'Nonsense!' 'Thy note, that forth so freely rolls. With shrill command the mouse control.'

Entrepreneur

February 2nd

We are in turmoil, which makes a change. Local tomato-growers are asking for planning permission to turn their acres into a Constable theme park. It will only need three-quarters of a million visitors a year to make it viable. There will be restaurants, carparks, playgrounds, toilets, everything you need for a day in the country. 'But where will they get all the Constables?' we ask. 'Aha!' reply the tomato-growers. To the further reality of everything they will offer being already here, the wild flowers, the woodland, the creatures, and most of all 'those scenes which made me a painter', as the great artist confessed, the theme parkers say, 'But what we propose is a marvellous business-like arrangement where you can enjoy all this without having to traipse along old footpaths, getting tired and muddy and all that.' Once, walking in Langham, the next village to that of the tomato-growers, John Constable told his wife that this countryside reminded him of Christ's saying, 'I am the resurrection and the life.' It was springtime. And very soon it will be springtime once more, and the modest river will flow slowly to the North Sea, now and then pausing, as it were, to reflect some of the most celebrated views in English art, the Field Studies Centre at Flatford Mill, the nature reserves properly cared for by the Woodland and Wild Life

Trusts, the ancient East Anglian towns and villages where both Constable's and Gainsborough's families made their living through which another kind of river will stream, that of theme park traffic. Hence our yelling in the lanes and waving our kalashnikovs.

By coincidence Ian and I found ourselves in Mistley the other day where an eighteenth-century attempt to turn the Stour estuary into a spa quite failed in spite of Robert Adam being commissioned to design the church. It was bitterly cold and scores of swans were grooming themselves on the bank. The wind blew in from the Arctic, and old ladies, wrapped like Innuits, dropped correct swan breakfast onto the surface of the water, where it was scooped up by whirling gulls. Mr Rigby the spa entrepreneur saw himself as the provider of a rivery theme park for the Quality. There would be fashionable sermons in Mr Adam's church, promenades along the Stour, carriage outings to the coast, though avoiding Harwich, of course, and meetings of the best society. But it all came to nothing, or near-bankruptcy, which is much the same thing. We actually went on to Harwich to see Captain Jones's house. It was he who captained the *Mayflower*. We stood, to, in wonder before the Electric Cinema, 1911, listening hard for the sound of Tom Mix and Mae West. One shilling this side, sixpence this side. An old man came to tell us that during the war he was let in free. We walked to Dovercourt, getting colder and colder. Vast ships crept into harbour. Below us was the seaweedy strand where Dr Johnson saw young James Boswell off to Holland after making him say his prayers. Boswell watched his new friend until he was out of sight.

On Sunday I preached on the Presentation, morning and evening, in one church then another. On those old watchers Simeon and Anna. Trevor, a teacher from Holland was present at both services. The ringers attempted a quarter peel. Constable's uncles and aunts and cousins slept in the table-tombs in the graveyard. I imagined them by the river, hard folk making a living, and the labourers digging yet one more great ditch, it being February.

At Long Melford

February 11th

The north wind doth blow hard against the north wall, booming and hooting in the ivy. What a treat. I wake up especially to listen to its ruthless old language, song even. And of course, now that James the chainsaw fiend has laid low the elders and willows the old farmhouse is open to its trumpetings once more and giving as good as it gets by way of chimney music. 'What a night!' we will exclaim the next day. At breakfast I congratulate myself for not allowing James to coppice a particularly fine stand of hazel because it is creating a kind of openwork Coromandel screen for seagulls. Blown in from the coast, they are black against the sky and white against the hill, and glorious between the interstices of the waving hazel. Snowdrops are everywhere, having, as they do, gone for long walks over the years.

Long Melford on Saturday to give a lecture on Edmund Blunden. I recall him chiefly for his sensitivity towards a young man who aimed to become a writer but was not able to say so as we waited for the train on Colchester station. He was a small, restless figure with – I told my audience – a face similar to that of an aged John Keats, if one could imagine such a thing. Blunden, after flying about the literary universe from Oxford to Tokyo for many years, had come to rest in Long Melford in the mill-house which Siegfried Sassoon had given him. Rich poets should always give poor poets houseroom, and where better than in sumptuous Long Melford whose grandeur should be enough to stop the traffic, only it doesn't, of course. We are in a fine Victorian village school, the one Gran would have known, having been born here in 1860. The Rector being present, I described her confirmation in c. 1874 by the Bishop of Norwich, his see taking in the whole of Suffolk and Norfolk. How, resting his hands on a purple-covered board held at each hand by the churchwardens, the three of them strolled up and down the enormous aisles to hopeful organ blasts, the packed boys and girls from miles around bowing their innocent heads were confirmed in the faith they had learned by rote. Outside on the green flapped a vast marquee bursting with tea.

Opposite stood Long Melford Hall, all orange Tudor-brick fairy tale, visited not only by Queen Elizabeth I but Beatrix Potter, a scarcely less formidable woman.

We drove home under gale-torn clouds which promised another roaring darkness. Caught among the trees, the telephone wire brought witch-like cackles which made talk impossible. It was in this February hubbub that I somehow managed to contrive a sermon on Lenten silence. Give up noise for Lent, I advised whilst the church on its rise above the river shuddered and shook, and the yews moaned. The old people in the nave might have protested, 'But you know how quietly we live!' And indeed I do. For the troubled, lonely Christ the silence of the wilderness allowed in the kind of talk which could not have been heard in the silences of home and synagogue, rare enough though they must have been. Human love and social religion would have kept it out. It was terrible to listen to, this voice with its rational alternatives. We sang *Benedicite* as we always do in Lent. 'O ye Winds of God, bless ye the Lord, praise him, and magnify him for ever!'

Winter Scents

February 15th

B itter, bitter cold it is. Grandmother would have said
that she was frawn – Suffolk for frozen. North-easterlies
cut through the hazels and howl in the barn. Birds are blown
about all anyhow. I check the oil. The white cat sleeps in the
in-tray to keep the letters warm. Snowdrops and crocuses
cheer up the churchyard, profuse, perfect, the latter smelling
of honey. Various attempts to heat the church have a moder-
ate success. Mostly they bring out dormant scents in the
woodwork, the frontals, the hymnbooks, those choir-robes
which haven't processed up the aisle for ages.

I am in this olfactory state due to Jenny Joseph ('When I
am an old woman I shall wear purple') having given me her
book *Led by the Nose: A Garden of Smells*. Although I have
another writer friend who has a habit of sniffing a volume
as soon as he opens it, and is the kind of person who gets
high on paper, I must agree with Jenny when she says, 'I
remember going to look at fabrics in a shop with a friend,
and she was ashamed of me because, while feeling a particular cloth, I smelt it. The nose is a useful means of information . . . but smell is a bit of a taboo subject still. I think
of gardens and the life beyond them in terms of smell.' And
so do I, only I hadn't realized this until I read *Led by the
Nose*. It opens the flask and lets out the gamut of fragrance

and of reek, the entire grammar of the nostrils as taught by plants.

Scripture is heady with incense from Exodus to Revelation. It starts with Aaron burning 'a perpetual incense before the Lord' and it concludes with St John's angel casting the censer filled with heaven's fire to us on earth. Incense is strangely warming, I find, although we are not High enough to have it. But as an experienced church-crawler from boyhood on, let me assure my readers that the merest remnant of what the thurible threw into the wintry chancel has a way of taking the edge off a freezing interior. When Moses set up the tabernacle, part of each princely offering to the altar was a golden spoonful of incense, a holy odour created by firing resin from gum-trees. Centuries would pass before Christian altars were similarly scented. The Tractarians adored it, perhaps because their crowded naves might have emanated mothballs. Exodus says that incense is for sacred places, not for human bodies. But it gives God's recipe for the holy oil for the flesh, and enchanting it is. We have to make 'a confection after the art of the apothecary' out of 'pure myrrh, sweet cinnamon, sweet calamus, olive oil, onycha, galbanum, stactes'. The ingredients run on, he knows alone what plants of his are required to repress the everyday reek of even the best of us. However, now and then some young man diverts this blissful substance to his own happiness and in Proverbs we have him 'perfuming his bed with myrrh, aloes and cinnamon' and telling his girl,

'Come, let us take our fill of love until the morning . . . for the good man is not at home.'

During February Jenny Joseph is led by the nose to the strong clean smell of juniper, to dowdy bits of lavender which, amazingly, gives off what seems to be an everlasting pungence, to parsley crushed under the snow yet still breathing 'parsley' for all its worth, but especially to her crocuses: 'I dipped my nose as near to the deeply orange stamen as I could and practically staggered back with the scent of honey in my head.' Never having purposely smelled a crocus I hurried out.

How to Plant a Wood

February 23rd

A week of outside and inside activity on the grand scale. Cold February rain when we are outside, thin February sun when we are inside. First we go to Fordham where, in the pub, I receive the representatives of the kind City firm which has given the Woodland Trust a vast sum to buy trees for children to plant in the bare fields. There are over five hundred acres of them at Fordham and when we are with God this village will have returned to its pre-Saxon canopy of oaks and ash, its hazel rides and thickets and, who knows, possibly its elms. The Fordham children make a good start, damply efficient, small spades flashing, rabbit-guards rolling, teachers watching. Just up the lane is the barn where Selina, Countess of Huntingdon, connected her dissenting congregation with her views on Methodism under the Toleration Act of 1689. I see her followers beneath the dripping trees, some of the former rather impressive, for it was her plan to save the upper classes. One of her methods to make her mission viable was to create Anglican clergy her chaplains but a consistory court soon put a stop to this. How many chaplains did a peeress need? Sowing cornfields with trees would have puzzled her. Back home, I feel uncharacteristically weary, my wellies twice the size they should be due to mud, my Woodland Trust hat like a soggy hassock. The cat stirs on the hearth murmuring something like, 'More fool you.' Going out on such a day, she means. The afternoon birds tumble up and down in the rattling lilacs, the old house says, 'Come in, come in.' When the Ayrshire farmers emigrated to the Stour Valley before World War One, they joined the Countess of Huntingdon's chapel at Fordham, finding our churches too High, too fiddle-faddle. It was they who rescued our give-away farms. But they also did what we did, strolled along the headlands on a Sunday afternoon with a pocket full of acorns, now and then stopping to push one into a hedgerow. Trees as well as oats were a crop. Except one had to wait a bit longer to take it. Like a hundred years. Isaac Watts lived nearby:

How beauteous are their feet,
  Who stand on Sion's hill,
Who bring salvation on their tongues
  And words of peace instil.

Keep it simple. Which it certainly was not at the cathedral. For Dean James a glorious goodbye in St James's. This was the thin sun day. Ever since I was born, the sun, winter and summer, had caught the sugar-beet factory whenever I journeyed to Bury St Edmunds, but now it played on the new tower and completely changed the view. A single tower. Should anyone ask why men build church towers they should go to Bury St Edmunds. Not that even there they will find a practical answer. It is just that we have to take stone to a beckoning height. Or glass or gold – lift it up to function as a beacon. Dean James's entire ministry at St Edmundsbury has been dominated by this elevation of stone. He and I once occupied a kind of wire-netting cage to see how the builders were getting on. They were artists from the Middle Ages in jeans and helmets, gently tapping the carved blocks into place. The sun was hot that day. So now the cathedral puts on a show called Choral Evensong, the splendour of which has to be heard to be believed. It is 'Praise to the Holiest in the height'. The tower has come, the Dean goes – and not looking at all worn out. I sit in my stall daydreaming, as writers are apt to do.

Jasper and the Flints

February 27th

Sometimes it is a simple movement which does Proust's madeleine trick. That fluttering hand behind the hospital window, what did it bring back to me? Another old man waving to us from his bedroom as we walked to school. He slowed us up sufficiently to wave back. Like the Pope's his face was little more than a whisp of whiteness but the greeting hand retained its early identity. In those days the old watched and waved from their own windows until it was necessary to pull down the blind, not from the retirement home.

Bishop Christopher arrived to consecrate the new altar in the north aisle and I of all people had forgotten that it was George Herbert's day, so no 'Let all the world in every corner sing my God and King'. I read the long and sharp encounter between Jesus and the much-wed woman at Jacob's well, and the bishop brought this and Herbert's poetry together. An east wind howled at the door as we begged 'Lord Jesus, think on me', a hymn by Bishop Synesius, a fourth-century Christian who was all for the enjoyment of reasonable pleasures. In the vestry I tell Bishop Christopher that the Indian novelist Vikram Seth now lives in Herbert's rectory and we talk about *The Country Parson*.

Then chores, then Evensong, then one of those rare fragments on television which plays havoc with Time and which again sets alight a personal experience which, had I thought about it at all, would have been hazy and inconsequential. The programme was Ray Mears's *Bushcraft* and as he blew on his Stone Age tinder it lit up the lanky form of Jasper, long dead, alas, as he collected Palaeolithic artefacts down by the river, always a cold job, as those flinty fields could only be combed by his searching eye when the corn was low. He had a room full of them, stone weapons and tools and domestic aids, all set out for use. But they were not used, just handled and labelled. Ray Mears, instead, made fire, made meals, made clothes, made 'a life' with them. And it was not just the few decades of my own existence which shot away, but millennia. On this scale Christ was walking to Bethany last week. I picked up my only find from Palaeolithic Wormingford, a kind of oblong flint buffing tool with smooth recessed sides the better to hold in the hand. And I imagined hands exactly like my own and even a voice raised in a hymn or calling by the river to say that dinner was served and, it being so long ago, these things now being no time at all. The young man on the screen is ten thousand years old. Jasper, who found what he is making, was thirty years old. He was a curious, loveable person eager and stumbling in speech, wanting everything *now*. Could he have a bit of some plant? 'Yes of course, Jasper, but when it is finished flowering.' This wouldn't do. In a minute the blooms, roots and earth would be sliding on his car seat.

'Water it well, Jasper!' But soon he died. Quite naturally, they said. I rewrote an ancient Greek poem for his funeral and an Icelandic sculptor fashioned a white wooden bird for his coffin. He watched it fly into the 'crem' furnace. Live *now*, commands Christ, not yesterday, not tomorrow. It was what Ray Mears was doing on his programme. George Herbert too. And the people whose bones lie in circles by the river. Planes and cameras found them out.

Putting up for the Night

February 28th

Among the compliments which George Herbert heaps upon Prayer, colourful praise after praise, extravagant tribute after tribute, there comes one which takes me straight back to market-day in Suffolk during my boyhood. It is 'Heaven in ordinary'. He contrasts this meal with that of 'Exalted manna'. The 'ordinary' was the common table at an inn such as still existed in towns like Bury St Edmunds and Sudbury until quite recently where the local farmers had lunch after visiting the corn exchange on market-day. Herbert had mixed feelings about inns, wisely advising us not to 'take a house' near one. Poor Francis Kilvert's house at Clyro was so near an inn that he could hear the shouts and see drunks lying in the gutter. Herbert would have seen the Cambridgeshire and Wiltshire farmers – 'which are thick and heavy, and hard to raise to a point of zeal . . . and need a mountain of fire to kindle them: but stories and sayings they will well remember' – coming to market and being sociable at the 'ordinary' table. I can see them now at the ordinary lunch in the Suffolk Hotel, roaring away, having second helpings, totting-up the saleyard invoices. 'Heaven in ordinary, man well dressed.' At Cambridge Herbert was something of a dandy. At Bemerton he advised the country parson to have 'his apparel plain, but reverend, and clean, without spots, or dust, or smell; the purity of his mind breaking out, and dilating itself even to his body, clothes, and habitation'.

We are inclined to imprison certain writers and artists in some convenient for us single spot, but Herbert moved around a great deal more than we like to think, finding him so 'present' in Bemerton. But Essex, Suffolk, Shropshire and Lincolnshire saw him, as did Cambridge and London, a tall thin rider at the inn door. 'When a man is on horseback he knows all things' was among the proverbs he collected. Both he and his mother had made a delightful discovery, which was the companionship of Christ. Inside or out, there he was, the interested friend.

> All after pleasure as I rid one day,
>> My horse and I, both tir'd, bodie and minde
>> With full crie of affections, quite astray;
> I took up in the next inne I could finde.

31

There when I came, whom found I but my deare.
  My dearest Lord . . .

Of course. Who else? In another poem he perfectly encapsulates Bethlehem.

When he was come, as travellers are wont,
  He did repair unto an inn . . .

Of course, where else? Few inns are mentioned in scripture, which is odd when one thinks of the endless journeys which wind their way through it. Joseph's brothers, returning home with corn from Egypt, are staying at an inn when they find to their horror that the purchase money as well as the food is in their sacks. God confronts Moses in an inn to tell him what to say to Pharaoh, though not in the New English Bible; and the full hospitality of inns, so long as one can afford it, is revealed in the parable of the Good Samaritan. Else inns in those much-wandering books are at a premium.

With Jane Gardam at Aldeburgh

March 4th

On Monday, at about ten past three in the afternoon, the spring began. I was raking the winding paths I had made through the orchard when I felt and heard a resurgence in the landscape, in birdsong, in the air, as well as the merest suggestion of less bitterness in the weather. Wild daffodils, still in bud, shook round the apple-tree. The hunt was unseen in the valley but was whooping away, hounds and horn in full cry – after nothing. A hundred rooks speared north, the sun catching below their wings and turning them a black silver. Well, I thought, spring! I raked carefully between the butterbur (*Petasites hybridus*) rosettes, which the postman thought were early lettuces, and rolled up a fitted carpet of moss from the base of my Rambling Rector (*Moschata*) and carried off a mountain of dry debris, whilst idlers wandered by calling out encouraging words such as, 'Rather you than me.'

At Matins we sang the beautiful *Benedicite*, petition after petition, reminding nature to sing to God – as though it doesn't do so every second. It is the song which Shadrach, Meshach and Abednego sang in their decidedly unnatural situation. Did St Francis call it to mind in the garden of San Damiano when he wrote his *Canticle of the Sun*? 'O let the Earth bless the Lord'. These petitions were muddling around in my head as I raked, and when spring started.

To Aldeburgh, for this is not only the time of the turtle but of literature festivals. Far and wide they spring up. The North Sea is still piled up like a dull blue wall waiting to obliterate us, the Suffolk wind doesn't wait to pierce us through and through, the shingle continues its clinking and rattling, and the Jubilee Hall is open to our wisdom. To the north the Nuclear Energy Authority has laid a roc's egg of a dome at Sizewell. In a hundred years' time the conservationists will launch a movement to save it. To the south the marshes glint warily and are excited by water-birds. All is as it was. Novelists and biographers bend before the implacable conditions of the hard little town. The children's boating pond is a splintered mirror of ice. It was all home ground for me once, only in the olden days. There is where I propped my bike. There is Ben's house. There is where the sea came in. There is where I wrote a story. There is where I sat in church, staring around as usual. There is where I helped to sing Britten's *St Nicolas Cantata*. There is the shed on the beach where I bought herring which were still wriggling from the sea. One shilling a handful. There is where I walked and walked, making up tales. You would think that it had all been blown away long since. But some places have a climate that is a preservative, and Aldeburgh is one of them.

The only thing I try to give up in Lent is my fretfulness when I hear what other people are giving up. The truth is that we have no real tradition of fasting in the correct sense. I would have given up noise for Lent but there isn't much noise to give up where I live. But I fill my Lenten addresses with encouraging silence. I preach the uses of silence. 'Elected silence, sing to me!' I quote, although knowing full well that the poet was at that moment a romantic teenager seeing himself in a habit in a cloister.

Hospice

March 12th

I haven't said thank you for the good readers who sent me much needed musical instruments for our St Helena Hospice at Colchester. So huge thanks. They were just what the doctor ordered. A music therapist had been appointed – but with nothing to play on. Music may not heal the flesh but it does wonders for the spirit. A therapist may heal with medicine, art or music. The hospice movement goes beyond healing into the realm of death. Art and music do wonders here. My instrument collecting was crowned this week when I visited the lovely St Michael-at-Plea bookshop in Norwich and the distinguished player Beryl Antony gave our hospice her B-flat clarinet. I held on to it in the train among the happy footballers. Hospices are where people of all ages die and I thought of the astonishment of maybe some young musician over whom the shades were falling handling this gift and playing fragments of the great clarinet quintets by Nielsen or Mozart, and their therapy putting immortality, not death, into his head. All of us hang on to all kinds of usable objects which are no longer of use to *us*, top of the wardrobe stuff, as I call it. We should give them away where they are needed. The more valuable, the better the giving.

St Helena, the patron of our hospice, was a Colchester girl

and I suppose our proto-archaeologist. She was a Romano-British princess who became the mother of the Emperor Constantine – who made Christianity the official religion of the state. She stands dizzily on our town hall holding aloft the True Cross which she dug up in Jerusalem. Alas dear Cross, one suspects that it was not only Our Lord who was hung on that scaffold but many another beside. At this moment they are excavating the chariot race circus at Colchester, the first to be discovered in this country. I glimpsed it as I was being driven home from a funeral, an enormous affair emerging from the barracks playing-field where some eight thousand spectators could watch. A continuity of local sport almost from Christ's day to ours.

This is the time to watch the hares play on the top grass. No more coursing – and not much more cooking, for few of us seem to have a taste for them these days. It used to be a mighty dish. In my 1879 recipe book it begins, 'Skin and empty the hare', so I did not read on. The 'jug' containing the hare would have been placed in a dripping-tin filled with boiling water before it was placed in the oven, and baked for two and half hours. All the same, I am not converted to fast food. Meanwhile, high on the hill the innocent creatures go through their happy paces, free from our appetites, whether for that little scream when the hounds blunder in or for the jug. How pleased William Cowper would have been. And no longer need Keats's hare limp trembling through the frozen grass, but have a life, as we say.

Yesterday I smelled primroses in the cold wind, delicate, reminiscent. Yesterday too the first wild daffodils, the ones which Wordsworth saw, broke cover in the orchard. And the wild sweet pea, which David brought me from Italy and which I have now grown from seed, sprouted on the windowsill in little delicate tendrils which quavered when I passed. The delicacy and fragility of life, how does anything survive? Because God loves it, said Mother Julian, how else?

Doctor Nature

March 5th

A green sequence of natural, rather than supernatural, meditations preoccupies my early Lent, each following the next in the way dreamings do, and stimulated by exquisite March days. First to arrive is Richard Mabey's *Nature Cure* with its echoes of John Clare's experience and of our years of talk. To be healed by skies and fens and flowers and the knowledge of these things, how wonderful. Of course, there is nothing new in these remedies. There they are, just *being* outside, and free for the taking. I took some big doses an hour ago as I wrenched up nettle stalks and bird-cherry suckers from the edges of the top lawn and listened to linnets. How well I felt – still feel. But it is marvellous to have this well-being all set out in chapters and set to music in words. Alongside Richard's testimonial to nature, for there is always an alongside reading with me, I read another nature cure called *The House of Quiet* by A. C. Benson (1904). What good writers depressives are. I remember William Cowper. My love of his hymns sometimes creates grins in the choir. He was suicidal but nature in the form of vulnerable hares showed him a trembling world which his God sustained:

> Ye fearful saints, fresh courage take;
> The clouds ye so much dread
> Are big with mercy, and shall break
> In blessings on your head.

Cowper liked writing in his greenhouse where his current hare could play around in safety. He would be there when the frosts were over – 'When the plants go out, we come in' – and he preferred the natural history of Olney to smart resorts such as Margate which he likened to a Cheshire cheese full of mites. But A. C. Benson's *The House of Quiet*, the old book which fell out of the bookcase just when I was reading *Nature Cure* and murmured, 'Read me' turned out to be the work of a depressive at one remove. A great many confessions in those late Victorian years were at one or even two removes. Their authors invented scapegoats on which to pile their failings and feelings. Arthur Benson, the Archbishop of Canterbury's son, no less, and Master of Magdalen, Cambridge, was a depressive who used bicycle rides through nature to cast off the black dog. And they did. He and my friend Richard Mabey are healed by the same East Anglian flatlands, the one concealed by the etiquette of his day, the other gloriously open, but both beautifully descriptive of their regenerative property. Except that Benson is frightened by woods which for him can be 'near the confines of horror', also still water. He must have open country and running streams. All in all he reveals a large man with the terrors of a child still.

My third nature cure seeker has to be Richard Jefferies who is young but consumptive and far from depressive. He died aged thirty-nine in 1887, a Wiltshire farmer's son who, whilst not a Christian, possessed a vision of nature – which included his own body – which the poet Elizabeth Jennings believed matched that of Thomas Traherne. Richard Jefferies' *The Story of My Heart* is an exultant, unhidden paean to nature and one which accepts the naturalness of death. It is a hymn to joy and a dismissal of Time. Christ taught the disciples to live in the Now, to step out without a penny, to be alive – really alive. As does Richard Jefferies.

Ways with Words at Keswick

Mid-March

To Keswick for the literature festival. To get into the train at Euston and to remain on it until Penrith, what happiness. Nearby, a Scottish woman reads to her little son Oscar just loud enough for me to enjoy the tale. There is Staffordshire, there is Lancaster, there is Penrith, and there, getting out of a rear carriage, is the poet A. Alvarez waving his stick in greeting. And here suddenly are the mountains in their endless permutation of shadows. On a March day in 1801 Coleridge's small son 'Looking out of my study window fixed his eyes steadily & for some time on the opposite prospect, & then said – Will yon Mountains *always* be?' They were in freezing Greta Hall, I am in a snug hotel where snowy Skiddaw rises behind an enclosed swimming pool in which a novelist splashes up and down, making the most of this outing, for as everyone knows we writers tend to be penned up, as one might say, immolated from each other for most of the time. Now we mix and identify. So that is what Deborah Moggach looks like. After dinner Louis de Bernières stands up to recite 'What gat ye to your dinner, Lord Randal, my son?' 'Now your turn,' somebody insists, turning to me. But in the first place I am suddenly empty-headed and in the second place poor poisoned Lord Randal 'fain wald lie doon' and must not be disturbed. Also I am thinking how like Coleridge Louis looks, a large rumpled figure with a searching gaze.

With a couple of hours to spare before I give my talk, I make the most of Derwentwater, first strolling along its edge, then striding off recklessly towards a muddy wood where huge machines are doing a bit of felling. It comes on to snow and then to rain, and then both. I take shelter beneath a boat and take heart from Coleridge, although he was only in his late twenties when he climbed and skidded around Keswick, and he was so ill! How ill folk were then. Those authors up at the hotel, how healthy they look. He used his aches and pains 'as a Storehouse of wild Dreams for poems, or intellectual Facts for metaphysical Speculation'. I look at my watch and see that I have to be on stage in half an hour. But I have lost my way. The snowstorm has blinded me. I hurry along in the wrong direction. An old lady appears. She stares at my feet to see if my shoes are fit for a short-cut across a drenched hill, and they are, and in minutes I am at the Theatre by the Water reading from my novel *The Assassin*. Coleridge named his son Derwent after my lake. It means a river where oaks are common.

Then home to readings and music at Little Horkesley in a full yet cold church, for there come winter days in these buildings when their heating is no match for the determined low temperatures which they have inherited from the Middle Ages, and one might be cosier in the churchyard. The music includes Trevor Hold's settings of John Clare, who loved the Lakeland poets. I find it moving that all our storytellers from whoever it was who wrote *Lord Randal* to those who make their way to twenty-first-century literature festivals have seen the same scenery, breathed much the same air. Looked into much the same faces.

Just before Evensong a quarter-peal was rung for Henry and our new Priest in Charge and we sang beautiful words about going from strength to strength, and about nesting birds finding protection on altars, and about 'Through the hours in darkness shrouded let me see thy face unclouded', as we called it a day.

Mrs Mason Dies

March 16th

East winds all the week. Now and then powdery snow blows into a vortex of bitterness. We process to the grave-side, the flimsy-looking black suits of the young mourners and our robes whirling about in the cold. A thousand years of this grief on this sward, I think. Death remains somehow comprehensible, acceptable even from hospital to church, but not at this hole in the grass. It comes as a shock. The childish comfort of 'Now the day is over', written a few miles away, vanishes as the clay-stained canvas ropes lower the woman down, down, endlessly down, and the sons and daughters flinch from the sight. There is a visible reeling back. Graves are, well, earthy, cremation is, well, tidy. Red roses are dropped one by one. Only a few yards away, over the churchyard wall, is mother's garden. A perfect cottage garden, a Geoff Hamilton garden in which flowers and fruit and veg all rise together, and which gives us pause after every service, but it is of little help now. At the funeral I have read St Paul's wonderful peroration to the Corinthians, changing his charity to love, and Henry has said great prayers, and a piper has wailed 'Amazing Grace', and two medieval bells have ding-donged over the village, and a sea of cars has waited in the field, and I have dwelt yet again on death and on body and soul, on mortal life and immortality. But home to tea by the fire.

A letter from my friends Sue Clifford and Angela King who twenty years ago created that inspirational movement called Common Ground. They have written a book with the inclusive title *England in Particular – a Celebration of the Commonplace, the Local, the Vernacular and the Distinctive* which, I suppose, is more or less what my books are about. Their letter says, 'Here the frogs are busy, jackdaws are cuddling up to each other as well as the chimney-pots, and honeysuckle shows its eagerness to salute the sun. Isn't that moment before spring glorious!' So I go around Bottengoms Farm making sure that, in spite of the icy gale, spring isn't lagging behind in the Stour Valley. Carpets of unfrosted primroses and snowdrops, of winter-tolerant hellebores, and two blackbirds, two bullfinches, two robins and a rat all feeding together.

To King's Lynn for the Fiction Festival. The trains wander somewhat haphazardly – it being Saturday – through the Fens. Ely Cathedral rises from the black earth in its almost gauzy, fragile yet safe stone, sacred mountain made by hand. At handsome King's Lynn the Great Ouse gives me its sullen wink. In the Town Hall I talk about my novel *The Assassin* under the very eye of Sir Robert Walpole. It is about a bookworm who murdered a beautiful man who, they thought, was the ruin of the realm. But it is curious that when one has written a novel it seems no longer one's own creation but its readers' possession. I actually had to think hard to remember one of its characters. And the story itself was told to me when I was a teenager riding around looking at old churches. An ancient woman emerged from one of them and said, 'A murderer lived here.' The ethics of assassination – had the Hitler plot succeeded, would the plotters have been murderers? My assassin took a tyrant's life on the spur of the moment but the victim had been his boyhood friend. It was a hot August morning, not a fenny afternoon in late winter by the Great Ouse. And so home with the footballers and the mild blizzard.

Memory Maps

March 20th

March is the cruellest month but on the first day of spring I cry, 'Enough!', seize a rake and clear the Nut Walk, the bitter, bitter wind notwithstanding. This is called making a start in the village. 'Have you made a start?' How the birds sing! They have dropped nesting moss here and there. The horse-pond is giving me its icy grin. The primroses waver. A hare is dawdling its way to Lower Bottoms. It is light until six-thirty, and this before the clocks go forward.

It had been cold-going at the two universities, Cambridge and Essex. It was Cambridge for the Readers Away Day and Essex for Marina Warner's Memory Maps. Alas, my favourite sight during these March visits to Cambridge being the classy shrubberies along the Victorian roads leading to Selwyn College was denied me by this final blast of winter. Usually they were in starry bloom but all they could offer this year was a bare rattle. *Iris reticulata* stood proxy for them in the college garden. It was the fifteenth Away Day for us. Readers tend to get a bit lost in the general scheme of things and John Wood's creation of this Day continues to be a blessing. The Selwyn lectures are provocative, witty, non-parochial, coat-trailing, or should one say cassock-trailing, and pretty well done. We lunch in hall with George

Selwyn watching from his golden frame. In 1841 he had more or less single-handedly taken the Church of England to New Zealand, teaching himself Maori on the voyage. He also took his Tractarian ideas. At the end of the day, as an Epilogue, I said three old prayers he may have known. Outside the court was arctic, Blomfield's high walls giving small protection. I thought of young Thomas Hardy designing 1870 Education Act schools in Blomfield's office and their elevations getting all mixed up with Tess's lowly disaster.

Essex University was even colder. Jules, who had driven me to it, said that at two degrees it would soon be like summer for him as he was off to work in Labrador. Essex has the tallest brick buildings in Britain. They were specially put up for our Easterlies to have a fine old time round them. Then to the theatre to present our Memory Maps. Six of us had to make a spoken map which we alone had explored. Mine was a map of Thomas Gainsborough in Sudbury, his birthplace. It was the small Suffolk market town of my boyhood. In the market-place stood the artist on a plinth, palette at the ready, and wearing beautiful Gainsborough clothes. How he had raised my sights! The Americans had given our town this statue just before World War One. It shone above the naphtha flares of the banana stalls every market-day. Wherever a great poet or artist – or saint – had been born a double biography arises, the official and the native one. There were all sorts of Tom Gainsborough stories in my childhood which you would not find between covers.

These I told now, tracing them on my Memory Map. I walked in *Cornard Wood* and called on *Mr and Mrs Robert Andrews* at the Auberries. There, as was common knowledge, the stone cats on the tall gateposts changed places at midnight. I had been on nodding terms with Gainsborough's Uncle Humphrey, headmaster of the grammar school, and the sensible person who had packed his brilliant nephew off to be trained as an artist in London. I was respectful to Mrs Andrews's grandfather Alderman Carter whose huge tomb said, in Latin, 'This day a Sudbury camel passed through the eye of the needle'.

New Grass

March 30th

Now and then a casual remark introduces a lost vocabulary. Tom on the telephone from his farm down below says something about letting his Lincolns out onto the water-meadows, and I experience the sight of that glorious rush of animals out of their shed and into the new grass. For minutes on end they are transfixed by the spring air, waving their heads about and caught up in an unimaginable bliss, then they thunder about and make gentle cries, and their beautiful eyes shine in the new sunlight. 'But I must keep them in for a couple of weeks more,' says Tom, 'until the pasture is established. Otherwise it will be Mud.' If I think about the old inhabitants of my ancient farm they tend to have two legs. Yet for centuries it would have been the home of beasts. There are the ponds where the Suffolks drew up their drink, there are the ghosts of pigsties, there is the hill where the freed cattle leaped. But where are the sounds? Where that clamour, those chompings, those raised voices, that restlessness of warm creatures, that clanking of pails and ringing of chains? At this moment if one stood out of doors all that one would hear is Mozart on the record player.

Yet, take a wet walk and wild animals betray their presence. '*We* are with you still!' they say. Badgers have gone to a lot of trouble to undermine the track. Hares dance on the skyline, rabbits take cover. Owls call. Water birds sail on Mr Rix's new lake. Here is a fat dead rat and a thin dead mouse. Gaudy pheasants parade in the orchard. A stoat makes a dash for it. Rooks are patching up rookeries and soon the returning migrants will be building for all they are worth. But the grain store will not be a city of goldfinches. Frogspawn will look like grey tapioca beneath the marsh marigolds and, should I care to listen, I will hear eventually countless minute sounds, not to mention in early April the joyous blair of Tom's unimprisoned cows. Duncan's hens roam where they will but thousands of chickens scream unheard in an Orwellian gulag. I used to marvel at the obedience of farm creatures when I was a child. I mean, why didn't the cows jump over the hedge and walk to Bedford, say? Why didn't the sheep simply stroll away to some shepherdless hinterland? But no, they all stayed behind their hedges, terribly unsafe, terribly unadventurous, passive as those passengers on the Auschwitz railway – except that they could tell each other, 'We're in clover.' There are black lambs in the top meadow and dog-walkers in the green lane. The dogs are allowed to cover me with kisses. Some have swum in the lake and are soaking. Robins rustle. Pike stir below the bridge. But the animal army which made the farm work has long since trotted and galloped away into that animal heaven called Rest. Rest was the final word on many a tombstone too, for this was what its owner had had precious little of in this life. RIP. 'Come unto me and I will give you rest.' How people once laboured until, like John Clare's father, their bones gave way. But the resting animals became a kind of promise to labouring humanity who heard their breathing and saw their great bodies borne up by the earth. I have been explaining the lovely word 'mothering' to the children, and where best to watch it in action. In a stable, in a basket under one of those hooped houses where the pigs live, and very soon in the new pasture. Also, fathers do a lot of mothering these days.

The Widower's House

March 31st

This morning, the last day of March, I am bemused by the opposites of two visions, my own of a country parish in springtime, and that of R. W. Southern's of the old Christian world in his masterpiece *The Making of the Middle Ages*. I have a few farms, flowers and folk to hand, he has everything of significance during the years 972–1204 in his eloquent grasp. So I read on wonderingly between long walks in the sopping lanes, astonished by such fluent learning, and by the loudness of birdsong. Very necessary rains have dimpled the river all week and made the daffodils translucent. There are shallow lakes on the tarmac and there is white water in the ditches. The gargoyles no longer spout onto graves but have their torrents led to the ground via guttering – which would not have pleased Thomas Hardy, who liked a tragic splash or two. The glory is that I managed to cut all the grass for the first time before the deluge. It descends softly now, throwing up mists and rainbows. And just as it would have done round about Easter throughout Latin Christendom, no doubt, which Southern describes so knowingly. Thus I walk on, my head full of buds and popes, steaming horses and emperors.

I call on Harold en-route. He is about to go to hospital to have his leg dressed and is waiting for his driver. There is tea and naval talk. His ginger tom, never liking to miss anything, joins us. The rain takes a breather and a pallid sun looks in on us through the kitchen window. It is a widower's house, clean and tidy but missing an occupant. It is hard to put the finger on what it is that marks a widower's house, as against a widow's house, when the house-keeping itself has stayed up to par, when order and care have remained much as they were when *she* was present, but so it is, this obvious fact. Harold rumbles back to the war and I listen to tales of Tito, oil-runs in the Baltic, bobbing mines, lucky escapes and wild risks. He then finds pictures of the granddaughters who used to play in my garden but who are now doctors in uniform. They beam from the frame. Having washed up the cups, Harold tugs out a two-gallon glass container of his homemade grape wine to see if it is clearing, and it is. His vine is the child of my vine, only ages ago, and it too is grown up. It wanders all over the bungalow tiles, over everything within its ten-drilly reach and making a fine show. Harold reckons it is a Roman vine which has climbed its way from Camulodunum to us. It has small sharp grapes which do wonders for a fruit salad. Harold scolds his leg. How will he manage to rotovate, to drive, to climb an apple-tree? Or to get himself to the Eight Bells? What ancient friends we are, this 'goer', this young sailor in his eighties. In another room the television is doing what it does in the middle of the afternoon and the kind niece arrives.

I come home to read some more about 'violent saints', and how during the twelfth century Byzantium 'remained in western eyes an ever-deepening mystery which simply invited destruction, not comprehension'. And thus on as the rain returned, and the brilliant pages flew, and cold callers were gently rebuffed on the telephone. One big treat. The showers have bought my *Magnolia stellata* into full flower. A thousand pure white blossoms pour over the leafless boughs. Also, a single fritillary shows itself under a bush. It is named, they say, after a Roman dicebox, the kind they shook below the Cross.

Before Easter

The kitchen window has long been my Herbertian introduction to each new day. Its glazing-bars measure up both the physical and metaphysical prospects which lie ahead of the morning tea. At the moment the April sunrise is blinding, creating negatives of positives, such as turning gulls into blackbirds as they wheel above the roughly harrowed hill. And the hill itself has grown Paul Nash-like mystical elements and become broody. If I climb it, I will see a promising land, miles and miles of it stretching in the direction of the estuary. But those who dwell in this promising land, and who are staring over their breakfast at *their* hill crest, may be thinking about the glorious views in which I matter of factly exist.

The spring literary festivals continue. Only what does one do when facing a crescent of wheelchairs in a care home? The microphone is the same, the glass of water, the happy introduction, the brief notes and the slips in one's books, but this is all. The audience, however, is quite unlike any other that I have spoken to on this reading and chatting circuit. It is like a blighted field in which, here and there, some evidence of its former beauty and usefulness remains. Why on earth, I ask myself, should these dear souls be interested in the man who stabbed the beautiful Duke of Buckingham in 1628? Or (shifting swiftly to another of my books) in Mark ploughing a hill? Or in myself, if it comes to that? But I plunge on until 'Any questions?', and am longing to apologize for being so irrelevant to that stroke which nature gives us just when we are making the toast, say, or wondering whether we should walk to the shops today or tomorrow. The care home is the best I have seen and the staff a contrast to any I have caught sight of in my limited experience of the places where folk go to hobble out their remaining days. Large sons arrive. How could that whisp of a woman, trembling incessantly, have borne him? An ex-headmistress who had escaped Hitler via the Kindertransport is now a Franciscan, she tells me, which explains what I can only call her freedom. She has learned to live outside this world's restrictions long ago. Tall and smiling, she looks the years straight in the eye. Not for her the walking-frame. She steadies herself with an ash-plant thumbstick, like the one I have, and which John Masefield made on Boars Hill. I take it for a walk round the garden now and then, just to show willing.

The bishop arrived for a confirmation, his wife hanging up his vestments before the service, myself as his not over-efficient chaplain holding on to his mitre and crozier as he welcomed the candidates into the Communion, all five of them. Bishops, like policemen, are getting younger, I thought. Coffee in the north aisle, lunch at the vicarage, the bells crashing away. And now Holy Week. The Easter flowers have to come into church before the Vigil because who can decorate a church before the Easter Eight O'clock? But Christ would have laid in that profusion of herbs and spices in the darkness before his Resurrection. Over the hill, in Nayland, in the Roman Catholic church, they have shrouded the statues, and in Southwark Cathedral, where I go to meetings, the vast, thronged reredos hides behind what looks like an unbleached sheet, all its busy sacred people stilled and silenced. 'Forth he came at Easter, like the risen grain', we all sing.

'Where to?'

Maundy Thursday

Those of us who wait regularly for the bus or the train at some particular spot are drawn unbeknowingly into a meditation of it. One sees them, not talking after maybe the brief greeting, lost in what this spot provides and their own experience of it. I am waiting for a bus which I caught when I was a child en-route to my aunt's house. Once the conductor would shout, 'Chapel Corner' when it arrived where I am standing this morning in the cold spring rain and it would rattle to a stop at a ragged grass diamond to which nothing was done unless the roadman gave it a swoosh now and then. But today, I note, having nothing else to do, Chapel Corner is a kind of sign city, with often only myself as its occasional citizen. So instead of contemplating Duncan's flat field opposite and the little cottage which was the Lemonade Shop (a spoonful of yellow crystals in half a pint of water for a penny), I find myself counting all the things a village bus-stop must have, the latest being the elevation of the timetable from four drawing pins in the shelter to a fine steel frame on a pole. Nothing is too good for a timetable. Drawing pins are now reduced to supporting our flower festival notice and a picture of a fat lady who has slimmed. Or Stour Valley Jazz.

Foreign travellers search around for the Chapel, not

knowing that it can only be seen in our heads, like the rough grass patch at the Y-bend which ordained where we would disappear on foot. It was built of pale green corrugated iron in 1898 by the Primitive Methodists and it resonated when it rained, which they said helped the singing. Folk came to it from miles around. Poverty-stricken farmworkers had paid weekly pennies to erect it. Before this the Primitive Methodists, who had broken away from the main Methodists in 1811, and who were avant-garde in their admiration for Quakers and their allowing women to preach, had met in our village forge, a stage having been assembled over the forge itself for the preacher to stand on – and what better picture of salvation and perdition? Preachers came from far and wide. One of them defined a miracle as 'Something wonderful, like a newborn babe carrying a sack of flour up a chimney.' In 1970 the Tin Chapel was replaced with a smart bungalow. For a while the little lost congregation found refuge among the Countess of Huntingdon's Connection and then, when this chapel became a house, with the Baptists at Bures. Now, when they go to heaven, their funerals are at the parish church and we sing their redemptive hymns, 'Lord, it is eventide, the light of day is waning' and 'The sands of Time are sinking'. I remember these labouring folk as I wait for the bus, and how their crowded voices would have poured through the galvanized iron onto the raggedy green.

But to an inventory of bus-stop progress. First, and a true

blessing, arrived a strong shelter with a vast handsome bench engraved B. R. 1959, a golden wedding present from the Grange, and which was once packed with travellers who now go about in Four by Fours, etc. But then came vast direction plates, concrete bollards, stone kerbs, four yards of tarmac for wheelchairs, the spring planting of crocuses and daffodils, thirty miles an hour signs and every kind of hoisted up reading matter imaginable. 'Where to?' enquires the driver. 'The Tin Chapel.'

By the Deben

April 11th

To Woodbridge on a summer's day in April, the gorse on Martlesham Heath in all its splendour. The sight of English gorse famously brought the Swedish botanist Linnaeus to his knees when he saw it in its full golden bloom on Putney Heath in 1736, but Thomas Hardy, in *The Return of the Native*, described a community entrapped by it. Our ancestors lived and died in a localized flora which could play havoc – or heaven – with their character, and which made them either open moorlanders or shut-in woodlanders. The Suffolk furze sped by, the hot, sealed traffic impervious to its heady scent, nobody gathering its prickly branches to make brooms with which to clear the soot from winter chimneys.

I am with John, lawyer, yachtsman and fellow lay canon of St Edmundsbury Cathedral and we are on our way to the rivery town which was my capital for many years. There are towns on rivers and rivery towns, and there is a difference. The latter are where boats and tidal reflections get into the politics. The boats are like those cattle waiting to get onto the meadows after having been inside for months. A few bob about but most are still high up in their stocks. They are so white, so gleaming, so trim and bright that they look as though they could put to river with not so much as a dusting. But this won't do for the sailing fraternity, who in a couple of weeks will descend on them with every polishing material known to man. We look in at Everson's boatyard. It is one of those fragile, wandering sheds which you would think a spring breeze would carry off to Holland, but there it stands as always, smelling of oils and canvas and useful bits of this and that, of masts and defunct calendars, expertise and languor. There's no hurry by a riverside. John points out a nice little vessel called *The Rangoon* in which the royal family penetrated the darker regions of the Norfolk Broads when the Empress was alive. Or when Arthur Ransome was adventurous. It looks good enough for a further hundred years. Opposite lie the grave-boats of Sutton Hoo and the sandy farms, the wind-rocked conifers and the coastal lanes. Down-river lies Felixstowe and the sea. Once having got to a rivery town there is no reason on earth why one should go anywhere else, and we return to the car in some journeying confusion. Not many miles from here the Burgundian Felix and the Irish Fursey set about Christianizing the East Anglians who, as everyone knows, badly needed it. St Fursey in furze-land. And soon, well in a century or two, there would be a rivery king – Edmund.

John is interested in Bernard Barton the Quaker poet and as a thankyou for taking me to Woodbridge I find him a cheque signed by him in 1830. Barton worked in Woodbridge Bank and was the friend of Edward FitzGerald who sailed a boat named *The Scandal* – 'after the staple product of Woodbridge'. Barton was a prolific poet, FitzGerald has made one poem, *The Rubáiyát of Omar Khayyám*, suffice for his entire reputation. He saved most of his literary genius for the letters to his friends. For him the river spelled freedom from the land, as it does to every sailor proper. A day or two before, the talk was all about burial at sea, Henry the vicar having officiated at such a funeral and I told him what the Queen Mother said when she heard of Lady Mountbatten's wish to be buried at sea, 'She always did like to make a splash.'

But now we are home to a furze-less garden and a rivery village, and I plant more wild sweet peas from Italy, and a ginkgo tree which was surprisingly presented to me after the service.

An Ipswich Boy

April 16th

Taking Matins I am suddenly aware, yet again, of the reality of public worship being multiple private worship, each voice, each closed or wide-open eye, each kneeling form contributing to the whole. Many mouths frame the ancient Hebrew poetry as 'the voice of the Lord breaketh the cedar trees of Libanus', Sir John's, Marjory's, Roger's and the stranger's within our aisles. Though careful not to lose my place, I find myself making fanciful connections between Ezra's cedar wood for the temple and the Lord breaking the cedar trees of Libanus in Psalm 29. Could he be sawing them up for building material? And where, I wonder, is the wilderness of Cades which he shakes? Who else is wondering this? Perhaps they know (though I doubt it) and see it all in their imagination, the trembling desert with its dunes aquiver and its sandy creatures running in all directions. Will ponders Ezra in the vestry before the service. 'There are some difficult names,' he says. 'Never mind,' I tell him, 'do your best.' The psalm ends with the Lord remaining a King for ever, so of course we conclude with Herbert's 'King of Glory, King of Peace' and thus out into the springtime with brief Anglican kisses and car keys rattling. It is short and beautiful this 'worship', this joining in whilst staying single, and yet being a 'whole'.

The daffodils fade whilst the ramblers blossom. I see them clumping by in their great boots, woolly hats and gear generally. They come in tens with appreciative voices and a dog or two. Quite why they dress as they do is mystifying to someone who spends half of his life and most of the year outside in a jersey and jeans. I once guided forty ramblers through the Elgar–Piers-Plowman landscape near Malvern and still recall my astonishment at being met at the starting point by Captain Scott's polar expedition crew. The Stour Valley ramblers wave to me as they pass and presumably I would recognize some of them could I make out their shapes. They are the windcheater version of crusaders, people protected from all hazards as they walk to Wiston. You never know, moorhens can be fractious, Duncan's fields could shake, my plum petals might cling to spectacles.

Visitors come in droves and eat up all last year's Flower Festival cake. Lunches and teas topple into each other as concerts are arranged and parish matters squeeze themselves into a writer's life. I go on the train – twenty minutes to Ipswich to give a welcoming talk to the excellent new ecumenical bookshop at St Nicholas, strolling up from the station with the shoppers. Cardinal Wolsey was baptized in this church in 1475. He was born a few yards away at the entrance of the beautifully named Silent Street, the son of the local butcher. I touch his font, talk to the Bishop of Dunwich, think of Shakespeare's farewell language in his *Henry VIII*, and of the Suffolk boy who went too far.

Shakespeare calls him 'the great child of honour' who was 'though from an humble stock ... most princely'. The windows at St Nicholas come almost to the floor to create seats for 'the weakest who go to the wall', and I think of Tom Wolsey escaping to them from his father's shop to have a quiet read. He would have founded a college at Ipswich but the scheme collapsed with his death. His Oxford college did not bear his name, but was called after Christ. Downfalls haunt religion. 'He hath put down the mighty from their seat.' An old man, speaking of his son, once told me, 'He climbed too high, so he fell.'

The Writer's Voice

April 20th

Saul Bellow has died, announces the radio, so I rummage through my fiction to find a reminder of his genius, returning with *Mr Sammler's Planet*, a novel about an elderly Polish gentleman from Cracow in New York during the 1960s. He is half-blind so the author makes him only partly comprehending of what he sees as he wanders the streets. He carries with him some of the borrowed culture of an English clubman, his own fastidious Jewishness and the horrors of Hitler. As with many old people, having little to do, he watches others. Mr Sammler reminds me a little of the retired clerk in Charles Lamb's essay *The Superannuated Man* who says, 'I am no longer clerk to the Firm . . . I am Retired Leisure. I am to be met with in trim gardens. I am already come to be known by my vacant face and careless gesture, perambulating at no fixed pace, nor with any settled purpose. I walk about, not to and from.' Though needless to add, Saul Bellow's old man does not have a vacant face but one which carries no longer understood things.

Thinking of Bellow's 'All Americans are outsiders' reminds me of the writer's voice 'off the page' as it were. How different it is in many ways from other voices. The Archbishop of Canterbury has a writer's voice, and it is the writer's voice which has crept in throughout the Christian ages, disturbing statements and theologies. Amos's was certainly a writer's voice, although he would no more have claimed it than his official right to prophesy. The fact that he was no more than 'an herdman and a gatherer of sycomore fruit' could not invalidate his being a poet. He reminds me of Mother Julian calling herself an ignorant creature. The writer no longer apologizes for his voice, whether on the page or on the tongue, if only for the reason that he cannot do anything about it. There it is, the awkward or off-key though sometimes beautiful tone which can throw out what is being generally said and believed.

> The Only News I know
> Is Bulletins all Day
> From Immortality

wrote Emily Dickinson. But then she didn't have Radio Four,

> The Only Shows I see
> Tomorrow and Today –
> Perchance Eternity

she continued. But then she lacked BBC One. She went on to say that the only street she knew was 'existence'. How strange it is to exist – to *be*. And how nice too when I can weed out of the wind, Kitty the white cat helping me, and the April birds hollering away, and the bare trees rattling, and Gordon and Elaine driving from goodness knows where to take me to the pub for lunch. What an existence. And a book to write some time or other, and hymns to be chosen for Sunday, and green ponds to be admired. And quizzes to be avoided in the village hall, for there my brain packs up as it does when someone asks me to do seven across – 'You should know this clue, you being a writer!' Ah, if they did but know the muddle that is the writer's head, the criss-crossings of its existence, its beliefs and heresies, its strange convictions and sudden truths. Even if at this moment I am no more than a tie-backer of raspberry canes.

At Tiger Hill

April 24th

The white cat, who now spends the night in the study, is able to lean from a high bookcase and give my tangled mop a tug as I pass through the curtained rooms to where the Whiskas lives, just in case I might forget. After a ravenous breakfast she takes to the window to catch the dawn jogger at his rite, a watcher and a holy one without a doubt. And then, although I have provided an excellent catflap, she stands at the door for me to let her out. Carefully, just in case there might be wolves, she looks in all directions, then heads off to goodness knows where, and I listen to Canon Noël Vincent talking about the growing distance between the book-led and the Internet-led man. This is a worthy observation and necessary to believe.

Organists have been in the ascendant. First Meriel, usually as indestructible as the service itself, isn't well enough to play for Evensong, so what to do, the congregation seated? So I climb the tower to find Peter and whisper to him through the clamour, then read his lips. 'Yes.' Soon we are rollicking through Charles Wesley's happy 'And can it be', reminding me of a boyhood evening at Mousehole with the Methodist fishermen, pints in hand, singing it across Mounts Bay, and glow-worms lighting me along the cliff path. Organist number two was David Drinkell, whose parents arrived to tell me how he is doing at St John's Cathedral, Newfoundland. Wonderfully, they say, producing an e-mail to convince me. But then he was the organist of St Magnus, Orkney and is the disciple of far-flung church music. His wife Elspeth is Orcadian and he says that once you have lived there the call of the northlands gets into your soul. I see him at Wormingford, ringing bells, playing introits, lifting the worship. Then – there is no end to this organist business once it starts – David Kinsela arrives from Sydney via Paris, where he has been giving recitals. All this in seven days. And now I must ring Christopher with the hymns for Easter Six, that pre-Ascension day, for as Mrs Alexander wrote, 'And ever on our earthly path, a gleam of glory lies.'

We have also held the annual bluebell party at Tiger Hill. It was warm, almost at times hot, and a nightingale sang half his song, breaking off midway as if rehearsing. About thirty of us, counting the children. I observed yet again how small children grow listless at picnics, lolling against father, longing to go home. 'But we've only just come! Sit up. Go and find the others!' The bluebells carpeted the woodland floor in their millions, a kind of electric blue which misted into a blueness which was beyond botanical description, verging as it did on the paradisal. We devoured egg sandwiches and wine, squishy cakes and tea, and now and then ventured into the bluebell ocean. Or sky. The picnic spot was guarded with banks of alkanet, a plant of absolute blue, though despised – 'You can't get rid of it!' I was sorrowful to hear this. It reminded me of the woman in Thomas Hardy's novel *A Pair of Blue Eyes* who complained how she hated a plant which neglect wouldn't kill. 'Look,' I said, turning to my fellow sandwich-eater, 'alkanet.' 'You can't get rid of it,' she replied. Alkanet is Arabic for henna. Would this abstruse information convert her to its delights? Hardly. There is no more severe sheep-and-goats ruling than that which defines the acceptable and non-acceptable flower. *Pentaglottis sempervirens*, how fair thou art in my beloved's bluebell wood.

Common Worship

May 10th

The great ash over the horse-pond is still no more than a tall tangle of sprouting sticks, whilst the twelve oaks by the boundary ditch are in full leaf canopy. The May skies are capricious, battering us with hailstones one minute, casting us warm looks the next. No sooner is the grass mown than it grows an inch before dusk. Late blossom and the first roses scent the chilly air. Some gadding. Alan and I show a friend places we know backwards and do our Pevsner stuff. The ancient lanes twist through the fields, their corners hidden beneath campion and cow parsley.

Richard Mabey calls the latter 'Arguably the most important spring landscape flower in Britain', and who could dispute this? *Anthriscus sylvestris*, you make the roadsides a wedding all the way. Nettles are at their best. As for the far rectangles and squares of hard yellow which the farmers have laid into the landscape with what must have been a palette-knife, well we can only grieve that the Impressionists missed oil-seed rape. It being the fashion to loathe it, my companions eye my pleasure warily. What will he say next? And thus to the home country of Polstead, Shelley, Kersey, Lindsey, Boxford, Assington, the land of teenage bike-rides and private adventures and self-discovery.

Now and then, in a neighbouring church, I read the 'Pray for' messages which are tucked into the board at the back, feeling that I am invading private territory. Ball-point petitions. 'Remember Geoffrey who has not long to live', 'Pray for Vivienne who has worry'. A woman could have stood on these very stones and written – if she could – 'Jesu, return my love from Jerusalem'. Early evening, so we pass the returning commuters, they and us politely edging into lay-bys. There should be nightingales but we don't lower the window because it is as cold as Christmas. Then back down the track with groceries and church-guides and tomato plants, our heads a muddle of flushwork and broken bits of the Reformation. We will take our friend in the other direction next time. 'How huge today's service books are!' we recollect. Hymnbooks for giants, prayerbooks in which we go backwards and forwards on Sundays. Here on the shelf where they have mouldered for decades is a splutter of Bibles and BCPs with broken backs and loose leaves. Corinthians coming before Exodus, Matins dropping palm crosses and pre-war calendar texts. Fly-leaves belonging to the dead. Gilded initials, even a coat of arms. And nice morocco smells. So what to do? Put them all back. How small they are, how perfectly hand-fitting and pocket-filling. Nearby is a glorious facsimile of a Book of Hours, all gold leaf and azure, with prayers bordered by toil and gardens, sports and festivals. Should the lady have carried it to church it would have entertained her during the sermon.

The shops are not busy, they say. One can feel this as one wanders through the local towns. There might be an excess of them, I think – knowing nothing about them. Or could it not be that each of us have what they sell and are making it last? The middle-aged are certainly pension-scared all of a sudden. The young, of course, knowing that they will live for ever, go clubbing. To them the VE Day celebrations are like remembering Agincourt. They talk to me at the University, and it is a lesson in reverse.

Going to See Traherne

May 20th

To Hereford to talk about Thomas Traherne, 'the master of the affirmative way which pursues perfection through delight in the created world', as Anne Ridler described him. Traherne has lain low for ages, just now and then raising his head above the religious parapet to bring his special gloriousness to Christ. The train crosses wide England from the Suffolk border to the Welsh border, and so far as I can see not a stroke of farm-work is being done all this distance. Just silent pastures and fields kept in order by the fairies. Nobody about, not even a fat white woman in gloves. Just land. Old churches bob in and out of view. Rivers gleam. Rain and sun take turns to weather the may trees. Where are we? Can this be Oxfordshire? There, hurrying by, is the ancient house in Kingham where robins had breakfast on the draining board. Richard Birt, the undoubted master of all that has happened by way of recognition of Traherne in his own country, awaits me on Hereford platform, plus those extraordinarily kind hosts who take visiting speakers into their houses without references, providing beds and toast and wine, and the run of their bookcases. And thus to Credenhill on its eminence, with the Black Mountains burning in the west. It was from here that the youthful rector looked out, his heart bursting with gratitude for God's hospitality to men. Not knowing any better, for he carried his infancy with him all his brief days, he could only cry out such thanks as,

> O mine of rarities, O kingdom wide!
> O more! O cause of all! O glorious bride!
> O God! O bride of God! O King!
> O soul! and crown of everything!
> I am his joy, I am his image, and his friend,
> His son, bride, glory, temple, end.

And so are we, did we but know it. Between talks I explore the churchyard. It too tilts and wavers on a higher plain. It says, cling on to life – have vision – give yourself a treat. And don't forget, says Traherne, what you are looking at is but the frontispiece to heaven. But he knew how moody a day could turn. 'Another time, in a lowering and sad evening, being alone in the field, when all things were dead and quiet, a certain want and horror fell upon me, beyond imagination. The unprofitableness and silence of the place dissatisfied me', and I was reminded of Bunyan, a guilty young man in the fields of Elstow going briefly mad because he thought he had committed a sin which was outside forgiveness. Not so Traherne. He took 'the dirty devices of this world' in his natural stride, denying their ultimate corruption, as one would a mess on a footpath. And of course, like most people in seventeenth-century England, or anywhere else for that matter, knowing that one would be an old man at forty, he had got going early in order to get everything in, the blissful countryside, all the words of the appreciative soul, all the best views. Was there ever such a flow of thankyou as Thomas Traherne's?

Evensong in Hereford Cathedral, just the choir and us. A Morley anthem. The arms of the stalls rubbed smooth by centuries of hands, including Traherne's. 'Love is the darling of God,' he told his pupil-friend Susanna. I am so busy thinking of them both that I miss the Lessons.

Talking of Towers

May 25th

The Ascension, like all the great feasts, lasts for longer than its day. Thus I can contemplate its mystery for days to come, and mysterious it continues to be. Theologians, no doubt, will have precedents for what occurred and these are not likely to include that of the witch of Endor who told Saul that she had seen gods ascending from the earth. Jesus left the earth where it had been its most hospitable, Bethany, leaving his friends looking upwards until the cloud of un-knowing intervened. I have sometimes been comforted by the title which Flannery O'Connor gave to her collected short stories, *Everything that Rises must Converge*. The convergence of divine and human love, well there is nothing cloudy about this. It is as plain as your hand before your face.

It was not all that long ago when the highest we could ascend was a tower or a mountain, a tree or a cliff. What was this to the ascending lark? A poised collection of these incessantly singing creatures seems to be suspended by the intangible nature of their song over the great field leading down to the farm. Although clouds are absent these birds are still too distant to see but their voices are magnified by space. Vastly higher still, one a minute and pretty well soundless, the Stansted planes come and go. Joachim, returning to Berlin, glanced out and down, and there for a second was where he had said goodbye, Bottengoms with its giddy willows and low-slung old roof.

Quite a few years ago now the medieval tower at St Mary's Bildeston fell into the nave on – Ascension Day. Hidden below the neat plaster were the cracks caused, they reckoned, by wartime bombers from neighbouring airfields. The congregation had been singing 'And ever on our earthly path/ A gleam of glory lies' when whoosh, what had been Perpendicular for centuries was a mountain of rubble. Everybody had gone home and only the brass couple were left looking up. What to do? Telephone John Betjeman. 'I am laid low,' he said, 'ring Ronnie Blythe.' Thus it was that I stood in for him on *This Week's Good Cause*, doing my best to wring hearts and wallets. I forget what we raised, enough anyway to make order out of debris. Had it been 1377 the local seers would have been striding around Suffolk, their fearful gaze to the skies, for like Nineveh, that great city, Bildeston had fallen, had sinned. Now of course it is all up to the diocesan architect.

Eating out has begun. We sit beneath the budding ash for lunch and under the leafy oaks for tea, following the sun round. Old snapshots show meals long ago. Tablecloths then, and laid places. And women toiling and men loafing. And cats looking on. And half-cut fruit cakes and a brown teapot. And spring shadows. And two boys on a branch looking down from far above yon azure height, and a book open and fluttering on a wall, bringing to mind the Gospel pages being whipped by the breeze on the Pope's coffin. Where shall we sit today, in the sun, out of the sun, and how long will we last, and have you brought the camera? These are as a matter of fact Thomas Traherne days when one should lie full-length on the earth looking up through the leaves at the blueness of the heavens and do absolutely nothing until God calls. The new grass is cold and delicious, and I can hear the horses cropping it.

Early Haymaking

May 29th

It comforts me somewhat that it is the youthful commuters who now talk about haymaking and cows, putting hedges back and seeing sugar-beet leaves take a shine after a good rain, and not the old farmers. When the commuters arrived we all thought that they would put the acres which went with their fine houses out to foster-care. But no. A number of them dash home from the City to feed stock before settling to hear how wicked their children have been in their absence and what is for dinner. Occasionally, if one is lucky, it is just possible that an actual farmworker might be spied during the hours when they are away totting-up immense figures in Bishopsgate, but generally the farm waits patiently for its owner to return, put on his jeans and comfort his cattle. Tom said that he had spent the spring holiday cutting his hay and silage – some of it in the riverside pasture which is still called 'Constable's' on account of it being owned by the artist's uncle before the Napoleonic wars. This haymaking ended perfectly in heavy rain which penetrated the shorn ground, polished the blue-ish ears of corn and pounded the willows. Rushing through it, I glimpsed a drenched white cat quietly observing sporadic lightning from a drowning wall.

Later, in the post-storm stillness, I walked to Hugh's to hear the result of the Flower Festival. We do not put on this yearly show for nothing. No Flower Festival takings, no quota. To think that the diocese's economy rests on such arrangements. This time the theme – there has to be a theme – was islands. So during *Songs of Praise*, standing between the school's lusty Treasure Island and Pip's cool Iceland, I read 'No man is an island, entire of itself, every man is a piece of the continent, a part of the main.' But when I came to 'if a clod be washed away by the sea, Europe is the less' President Chirac was the man who came into my head. St John the Divine on the Isle of Patmos dislodged him. We sang hymns which were clearly entire of themselves, their once immense messages half-lost in favourite tunes. Then we loaded up the takings, switched off the lights, locked in the scent and left all this floral ingenuity to get on as best it could with the grey severity of the pillars and the blackening painted windows. Waiting for the key to turn in the lock, I heard the clock go clunk. A kind of that's that. The table-tombs of the Georgian farmers and millers, so useful for the flower arrangers' sandwiches and wine, were resuming their well-lettered dignity, and the churchyard trees were all standing to attention and getting ready for their secret night-life.

As May crosses into June we are to read the Book of Ecclesiastes, that matchless confession of world-weariness, although how anyone can be world-weary when the days are at their best, heaven only knows. The Preacher wraps his gloom in such marvellous language that he somewhat undermines his conclusions. When he complains that there is no new thing under the sun, I – at this pre-summer moment – can only ask, 'Does there have to be?' Reading on, disillusioned or not, who can resist this enchanting writer? He is the man who had everything but who is now an old man for whom everything has turned to dross. He venerates sadness and makes it beautiful. Yet at the very end, just before the silver cord is loosed, he finds the light sweet and the sun 'pleasant'. As shall we all.

Albert Campion and the Green-winged Orchids

June 4th

Pentecost-Whitsun, an unmissable date on the calendar, for this is when we journey deep into the Albert Campion country to pay homage to the green-winged orchids, thousands and thousands of them flaunting their purple in a ten-acre meadow. David leads, of course. He is the priest of wild flowers, their advocate and protector. Hardly a week passes without him and Joe the spaniel arriving at the door with botanic tidings. He is single-minded and should I throw in a bit of unbotanical information en-route to where he has sighted a patch of wild clary, he drives on like a silent angel, not chiding me for the interruption, but flatly uninterested in what I am telling him. Which is as it should be. However, the green-winged orchids being so near Albert Campion's land, he takes me to it and we unsuccessfully search Tolleshunt d'Arcy churchyard for his creator's grave. I glimpse Margery Allingham's house. It is the kind of house in which one of the Queens of Whodunnits should have lived, and with a butler to open the door.

> There are, fortunately, very few people who can say that they have actually attended a murder. The assassination of another by any person of reasonable caution must, in a civilized world, tend to be a private affair.

Exactly so. And Mr Campion with his pale blue eyes would have agreed. And now David and I are out of shot of that inspired Remington and back to flowers and first swallows, and the tantrums of those who do not wish for a strong root of clary to see off the mower in the churchyard, meaningful plant though it is, for did not our ancestors translate clary as 'clear-eye', even going so far as calling it, very grandly, *Oculus Christi*, 'Christ's eye'? David has persuaded Fordham Church to leave a patch of it by the wall and we stop to pay it homage. When we put the matchless rural poet John Clare in Westminster Abbey a few years ago, the sculptor made play of his name by carving a sprig of wild clary. Look for it in old, old graveyards, *Salvia–Salus–*health. Its huge roots go down to the dead.

Before this we walk the green-winged orchids meadow in a chilly dancing wind which vast hedges fail to keep out. Here I must explain something which Albert Campion would not have cared to know as he searched for a motive. Which is that *orchis* is Latin for testicle, this defining their tuber-like roots. These multitudinous green-winged orchids which dazzle our gaze at this Whit-Trinity moment are *O. morio* – 'fool' orchids because their perianth segments come together 'like to a fooles hood or cocks-combe'. Which makes them newsworthy. Perhaps the government should do something about them. Tall buttercups and tiny adder's tongue break up the distant purple with Monet-like skill. How can we leave this old meadow, wind or no wind, tea or no tea? This damp sward which articulates a previous understanding of the countryside better than any book, that is if one knows a smattering of the earlier flower language and can follow its sexy drift.

Homeward bound, we meet the out-of-town shoppers on their way to worship in piled-high aisles. Crossing Abberton reservoir, David proffers something other than flowers. 'This is where they practised the bouncing bomb for the dambusters.' I imagined it doing ducks and drakes over the cold water. In the back, Joe the spaniel murmurs his car-song. 'He always does that,' says David.

Honorary Ringer

June 11th

There they stand, in the front row at Evensong, the Past Masters and Present Master of the Essex Association of Change Ringers. For have not they achieved a peal of 5,040 doubles in two hours and forty-four minutes? A board goes up in the tower to say so. I, an honorary ringer whose only achievement is to have tolled for the service, am humbled before them. We sing of the sacred minster bell which peals o'er hill and dell, and have our photo taken. I am well versed in peal-boards and do not like to see them skied where those who come after us cannot read their justified boastings. It is a soft pre-summer night and outside the limes are standing stock-still. Earlier on, I preached on Barnabas, Son of Consolation, whose real name was Joseph. He was the leader of the first missionary journey but was swiftly overtaken by Paul. They parted company over John Mark. Joseph-Barnabas and Saul-Paul were the first men to hear the word 'Christian'. It was said at Antioch, and noted by two Jews. Barnabas had led Paul by the hand and taken him to the apostles. It was the day of introductions and departures, of definitions and confrontations, of new names and discoveries. Only camel-bells would have rung out over these vast events. Past and Present Masters do not stay at home. In the worldwide freemasonry of towers they are honoured guests. But there are numismatic limits, as an eighteenth-century writer proved. Had our ringers tried the twelve bells of St Paul's Cathedral, say? Of course, they had been welcomed there. Although to ring all the possible changes on twelve bells would taken seventy-five years, ten months, one week and three days, reckoned the old bell-author. But what a peal-board!

Our bells spent their first four centuries in All Saints, Colchester, arriving at Little Horkesley in 1958. Those who listened to them most would have been the prisoners in

Colchester Castle, a notorious hell-hole. Among them would have been the Quaker boy-martyr James Parnell, a hero of my own youth. I thought of him whilst watching *Songs of Praise* from the Norwich Meeting House. A remarkably successful evocation of the life of Elizabeth Fry in which the hymns had not had the worship wrung out of them, as must happen in many much-rehearsed programmes. Parnell was a tiny lad who had talked with Fox and Whitehead in their prisons, and who had come to grief with the law when he preached outside various East Anglian churches – 'steeple-houses'. And thus hence to the terrible Colchester prison and from the road to which rang our five bells. A woman gaoler lodged him in a high-up recess in the wall and made him climb a rope to fetch his meals. He fell and died. The verdict was that he committed suicide. This was reversed. He was, like so many prisoners then, murdered by gaolers. They said that he would have been a great writer, another Bunyan, maybe. He was eighteen. But he heard our bells. All Saints, Colchester is now a natural history museum, and where James Parnell's grave was dug is now, on a summer's day, a corporation park for children, lovers, picnics, band music and meticulous flower-beds. Aged fifteen, he had written an essay called 'The Watcher, or a Discovery of the Ground and End of all Forms' . . . Were he living now he would have been following Bob Geldof around.

In the rose-crowded garden sometimes I hear the Horkes-ley bells and sometimes the Wormingford bells. But never at once, not due to the wind, but because the ringers cannot be in two towers at the same time.

Martin Bell Comes to Tea

June 20th

The heatwave is felt every hour of the day. It says, 'Meet me at midnight, at four in the morning, at noon. Whatever time it is, I make all things different.' Thus I watch the indigo trees in the small hours. They are still and smoky with mist, and full of singing birds. The corn is static and blue, the new reservoir a silver line. The white cat stirs on the garden wall but the white horses, monumental beneath the may hedge, show not the slightest movement. William Cobbett *rose* every morning at four o'clock! I tell myself – got up and wrote. But I stand at the window doing no more than looking out, which is occupation enough at mid-summer, and the warmth of yesterday collects around my bare skin.

It is baking hot when Martin Bell arrives, he in his white suit, his sisters smiling, and all of us talking about their father Adrian Bell, that unique Suffolk writer. Their childhood farmhouse can just be made out through my willows. Adrian Bell was not so much a literary hero to me as a boy, but his being an author made me watch him. When I told him this – a confession of sorts – many years later, he laughed and asked, 'What did you see?' What do we see when we watch writers? Of course, we know all too well what writers see. Very strange things if one is to go by their books. Adrian set the *Times* crossword puzzles when he wasn't looking at Suffolk and putting down the likes of all of us between the wars. He was a loquacious man who missed very little and who wrote wonderful prose. He called his son Martin because of the martins in the eaves of his old house. Should we not borrow more bird names – Jay, Crane, Bunting, though of course not Cuckoo. After the Bells have left I re-read some of Adrian's *Silver Ley* and I am twelve again and biking on a blazing day to Arger Fen and there are chalked boards outside the pub which say, 'No peapickers, no gipsies'.

It is late June and we are to remember St John the Baptist. Not that I ever forget him. I am sure that if I had lived in Palestine then I would have looked at him as I once looked at our local author, somewhat sensationally, and would have deserved that divine reproach, 'What went ye out into the wilderness to see? A reed shaken with the wind?' Prophets were not to be stared at but to be listened to. But Christ's herald would have been a striking figure by the water's edge even to those too far off to hear what he said, day after day, month after month, until his voice became intolerable for some and they put a stop to it. He was, said his cousin, 'A burning and a shining light' – which must be the most beautiful of all epitaphs. They named the hypericums after him, those flowers which are each a golden speckled sun and whose juices are blood red. A tall hedge of them bends across my path as I cross the grass, half-blocking the way and telling me, 'Not so fast!'

Old chaps sit in the cricket pavilion, drink beer and observe their young selves in the photos. Cricket talk is the chamber music of sport, winding in and out, requiring all one's attention. The speakers are deputy patrons of the club and know just where to come in. There were great authors who actually wrote this cricket-talk music down and got it published. The pitch itself sizzles and dogs lie panting on the crease. You could cook bread in the scattered cars. I write the Sunday services. Do we know Percy Dearmer's 'Lo, in the wilderness'?

Going to Beccles

June 25th

To Beccles to sign books on a blowy day. Through the train window I can see a yacht sailing on flat land, and munching cattle, and the low and lovely Waveney valley. Beccles, whose name suggested 'hooks and eyes' to the poet Edward FitzGerald, is 'all on the goo' as they say in Suffolk and Norfolk, it being Saturday. In the broad church, kneelers are being set out for the afternoon bride and groom. They will kneel where Edmund Nelson and Catherine Suckling knelt for their wedding, two young 'rectory' people whose third son Horatio would change English history. The bells are clamorous in their vast detached tower. Beccles is pitched on an escarpment above the barely moving river and is one of those little towns which breed great men. I sit in the Gazette Bookshop, signing away, devouring ham sandwiches, thinking of the Nelsons. Catherine's ancestor Sir John Suckling had written,

> The waving sea can with each flood
> Bathe some high promont that hath stood
>   Far from the main up in the river:
> O think not then but love can do
> As much!

Which sound to me like love in Beccles. Horatio Nelson saw these pantiled roofs, heard these bursting bells. Roy and Betty my Methodist friends come to watch me labour. We go back a long way and our talk of the dead winds in and out of the signings. In the undisciplined manner in which my mind works, I suddenly remember how Henry James resolved the problem of his heroine Nanda in *The Awkward Age* – she knew too much for a respectable girl – by sending her to Beccles, where she could live respectably ever after. Across the single-line station four tall spikes of mullin are marvellously yellow and wild flowers fill every crack in the concrete. Next week, Ely, Saffron Walden, Sudbury. 'Put to Paul', and so I write affectionately to strangers.

Mr Sycamore has levelled my farm-track. He does it every five years, slicing off the grassy rise and revealing generations of flints which women and children would have cast there from the fields. From being a threat to cars it is now a perdition for walkers. But be brave, soon, soon, there will be the lawns and roses, the coffee and the cat. All the talk is of hay. Never was there hay like it, says Duncan. Outside Peter's meadow, between signs which say 'Pekin Bantams for sale' and 'Honey for sale', is 'Hay One-fifty'. It stands in pale biscuits in the clipped pastures, hay such as you have never seen before, perfectly grown and cut hay, fragrant as dawn. But are there enough creatures to eat all this hay? I mean with grass growing fast all the year round, as everything seems to do now? Shall we have to ship it to Beccles, where those sailing marshes could be sodden in winter. Also among our roadside bargains is a nice little open sports car, one owner (Noddy?). For shoppers there is the village store, the supermarket and – the verges.

I am still deep in Hilary Spurling's *Matisse*, dreading it to end, sitting on the garden bench, regretfully turning its pages, worrying about Madame Matisse's health and matching up the artist's colours with my June mornings, my reading backed by the soft clapping of aspen leaves. I have also to read Sunday's lessons. How well they are read in all three country churches, how individually.

'The Assassin' at Dartington

July 13th

At Dartington once more for the writers' favourite litera-ture festival, 'Ways with Words'. It is where size mat-ters, not our size as authors but the amplitude of the estate, with its towering trees, world of lawns and hints of Dart-moor itself, the order it imposes on our bookish heads and lavish borders. 'What a treat!' we tell each other as we watch the novelists, journalists, poets and scribblers generally being debouched from Totnes Station. Our works sizzle under awnings and those who have paid good money to listen to us move through the great gardens like figures in an Edwardian painting, slowly, hushed, relieved of all care whilst the sun burns down. The heat has caused the sky to go beyond its July blue into a wavering pink, and straw hats appear.

I have been partnered with the Irish novelist Ronan Bennett. Unbeknown to each other, we have been stirring the religious embers of the seventeenth century, poking into them, making them flare up and cast a little light on what we may, or may not, believe today. There are history and theology proper, and there are imaginative forays into them, such as ours. Ronan looks Jesuistical but is decidedly not. What do I look like? It is not for me to say. But here we are on the dais in the Great Hall of Richard Holand, half-brother to Richard II, to answer for our audacity. Ronan's probe into the past is fearful in the extreme and all the comforts of Dartington fled as I read his story about the godly, as it was called, goings-on in a little Yorkshire borough in the 1630s. *Havoc in its Third Year* is a novel about recusancy, about how a Catholic family coped with 'godliness', about humanity and inhumanity, about mercy giving way to justice. There was a hive of recusants buzzing all around my house at that time, paying their non-attendance fines, harbouring priests and experiencing a fear which was no more than a word to me until Ronan aroused, in his novel, the 1630s knock on the door. He stands at the microphone and reads it in his soft Ulster voice, and history loses its charm, as it has to do when such searchers dig into its ashes. I cannot remember being so frightened by an episode in Christian history, and God knows there have been frights enough, and when I walk past the little church at Withermarsh Green, our recusancy centre, where – it says – the Mass has been celebrated without interruption from the earliest times to our own, I will know how those Stour Valley Catholics shook in their muddy shoes.

My embers are of the Arminian attempt to create a spiritual compromise between the godly and what a later hymnwriter would call 'the beauty of holiness'. For a few years it looked as though the examples set by Lancelot Andrewes, officious Laud, grim Wren, Little Gidding and Bemerton might heal the breach, might patch up the ruins, might set up a strictly loving Christ in his inhumane temples, but then came the Civil War. The anti-hero of my novel *The Assassin*, a young army officer torn between science and Faith, thought that the poison could be cured at the prick of a knife which he had bought for tenpence in a shop on Tower Hill – could be let out of our society and its rulers. His name was Lieutenant John Felton and he lived just up the road from me when I was a boy, only several centuries earlier. I waved to him from my bike, this bookish soldier whom they dubbed a 'malcontent'. But who can be content with 'religion' mal-used? Felton's friend, converted by Galileo, not Our Lord, pointed to the stars, looked up to the immensity of creation. What are we to make of our Earth and its minute role in the universe?

John Clare and the Haymakers

July 16th

Those places we visit but once a year have only one season. For the old pilgrims it was always spring at the shrine. It is perpetual July in Helpston when we honour John Clare, everlasting pre-harvest and constant blaze of midsummer flowers. The Clare Society meanders in his steps, though wisely boarding a bus to the poet's more far-flung haunts around his beloved Swardy Well. It is a fissured scene of pale stone and dried-out wetland, with stony tracks and evidences of toil. Here he met the gipsies who showed him how to play the fiddle by ear, and whose flashing-eyed women tempted him. My lecture is about his gipsies, Borrow's gipsies, Matthew Arnold's Scholar-Gipsey, and the Suffolk archdeacon who wed a gipsy. Also about us all having no lasting place. The Helpston children have surrounded Clare's grave with midsummer cushions – turfs stuck with flower-heads – and the Helpston pubs do a roaring trade. Morrismen dance in the baking road outside the Blue Bell. One day a year friends embrace. All is as it should be in a village whose calendar has a single page – July. Hollyhocks sway giddily, the birthplace is for sale, the barn in which John Clare did his arithmetic, figuring it out in the threshing-dust, has no more work to do. Peterborough commuters observe our annual invasion from labourers' cottages. I sit on the market-cross for a second or two, feeling the hot stone through my summer clothes, as did centuries of Helpstonians, their poet included, but having to impose his descriptions over everything to see what he saw. He was a list-making genius, putting down his Helpston to the ultimate bird and plant, creating a wonderful inventory of his village existence, including a tragic hymn, 'A Stranger once did bless the earth', which delicately touches on his own fate. 'Yet in lone places forced to stray' – he and the gipsies. Soon we are driving home in the air-conditioned car, belting along what was the Great North Road where

Clare had walked with bleeding feet, 'another broken-down haymaker', as a passer-by said.

Roger has been turning his hay – by hand! That is his 'rubbish hay', the border hay, thick with flowers which the locals call rubbish. Rubbish must be kept down, although, by calling it hogweed, nettle, ragwort – there is a current near-hysteria about this wild flower – I enjoy these towering July blooms. But a big hay year. Roger buys me a new, very light scythe to replace my massive Father Time scythe. I shall initiate it in the orchard once I have put paid to all this writing business. I shall let the 'rubbish' lie like all those ordinary men who 'fall' in battle the generations over, 'Peter upon Paul', as the World War Two poet said, for anything is a mighty slaughter, say what you will. Make room for regeneration.

Matins at Little Horkesley, a leafy world sizzling in the heatwave, the choir in mufti, the enclosed air delicious with wedding flowers. I preach on St Benedict and his bright sister Scholastica. He was a layman from whom there still descends for priest and laity alike the Church's best order-liness. Very little is known about him but it would take an army of scribes to set down his achievement. He said that his Rule was one for beginners, a school for those in the Lord's service 'in which we hope to order nothing harsh or vigorous'. His emblems are a broken cup and a raven. He and his sister share the same grave. It and all Monte Cassino would stand in the path of the Allied armies but the Rule

endured without a scratch. A true Benedictine asks no more
of life than to work in God's house on earth, and to be with
Christ anon.

The New Tower at St Edmundsbury

July 22nd

And so the great day dawns. For years a parcel of steel
and plastic thrust skyward over the town but now, to
change the metaphor, a living stone has shed its chrysalis to
soar upwards, giddy pinnacles and all. It was worth the long
wait. When we agreed to put a tower on the cathedral
we were not expecting this, the pale loveliness of it, the
completeness, the huge flushwork E for Edmund catching
the sun. And now for its consecration, even if the carved
Clipsham, Doulting and Barnack stone, and the knapped
flint declare their timeless holiness. It is a hot July morning
and the marquees are done to a turn. Women hide under vast
hats. Mayors clank their chains. The Prince and his little
Duchess are met with a fanfare. A man selling tenpenny flags
for a pound is sent on his way. A band plays oompah in the
Athenaeum porch to enormous crowds. Brad Pitt in a police-
man's helmet stops me at the west door of the cathedral.
'What is in my case?' 'My robes.' A likely story. He opens it
and fumbles around, then thanks me. We process in to:

Many a blow and biting sculpture
   Fashioned well those stones elect,
In their places now compacted
   By the heavenly Architect,
Who therewith hath willed for ever
   That his palace should be decked.

And I think of Habakkuk standing on a tower to see what God wanted him to do – it was 'Write the vision.' This was very difficult, although every now and then a writer manages it. We sing *Te Deum* to Britten and 'God is gone up with a triumphant shout' to Finzi. I can see nothing from the lay canons' stalls except other lay canons. Somewhere below us is an ocean of sound, remote, coming and going like distant tides in a conch shell. Processing out, my bands fall off onto the road. I snatch them up and tuck them back in. Only a thousand people noticed. By now it is blazing hot and the hog roast will be done to a turn. I imagine Edmund, crowned, they say, on the hill above Wormingford on a cold Christmas Day, aged fifteen, murdered at Hoxne aged thirty, and of the centuries of pilgrims come to see him. For many he would have been the only doctor for their illnesses. Would a visit to him make them better? His shrine would have been a milling out-patients as well as a delightful destination. It was there that the barons drew up Magna Carta, it was there that they tipped out his bones. Well, little King of the Angles, look how you have come home! How once again you tower over us!

Mrs Goff, landlady of the Angel, comes to talk to me about old times when her hotel was a literary venue. We stand in the Square, dodging enormous hats. The police pen us in with smooth hurdles. 'Back, back!' Only politely. Over there, on the pavement, we see free men and women, friends who can go to the Angel bar, who can do what they like, but we are prisoners for the Prince's sake. Hands stretch out to him as once they did for saints. Released without a stain on our characters, we head for the Great Churchyard where our car burns. But, alas, we are lost, lost among the St Edmundsbury-dead. Gordon thinks he too will die.

Full of Health

August 3rd

My pang of guilt when switching off a confessional illness. Not always of course, but usually. This morning it was motor neurone disease but then – I rationalize – the old friend will ring up tonight to tell me about her degenerative maculalutea, those yellow spots which are clouding the retina, so that the telly darkens and the car can no longer be driven and the world itself fades. And I will listen to the specialist's treatment and remember her once-sparkling vision. Or it could be news from a far country, Australia, about a cancer, or finding Helen, a century or more old, sleeping her last days away. People usually start on their ailments just when I am making an omelette. 'Is this a good moment?' they ask. 'Oh, yes,' I lie, being saintly. Should by any remote chance I wake up in the small hours, I devote them to prayers for the sick. Where sleep is concerned, they are less efficacious than counting sheep but saying them makes me feel useful. I recall an old neighbour, the wife of a retired country clergyman who, when I encountered her on the station platform the week following his death and asked gently how she was, found my conventional question crushed by her reply – 'Full of joy!' And how could she not be, with the slow dying past and her Arthur with God? At Ipswich we changed for the London train and I thought of his speedy transition to the *Jerusalem luminosa* in which he believed, although possibly smiling, rickety old chap that he was, at being endued 'with so much beauty, full of health, and strong, and free, full of vigour, full of pleasure that shall last eternally!' But that is the Middle Ages for you, when you went to heaven at thirty-five in pretty good shape.

I have just come in from being a few yards nearer paradise than is customary because of the ivy. It had no respect for the windows on the north wall of the farmhouse and had been gradually shutting out the light. They were the windows of John Nash's studio and when I used to chop this glossy growth he would sigh, 'Poor Ivy,' and wasn't a bit grateful. Dizzily aloft on the extension ladder, I tug it from the tiles. It comes away without a struggle, showering me with brick-dust and old nests. I cut a line about eight feet up and tell it, 'Thus far and no further.' Then I clean all the north windows and evening comes, and I trot down the silver rungs like a squirrel, amazingly filthy from what one might assume to be a neat task. But you know ivy. Indoors, I free a trapped bee from a pane by the renowned card and glass method, but would have slain a couple of flies. But I hear the voice of Satish Kumar, that great teacher of Life, saying like Blake, 'Little fly, who made thee?' and with infinite feeling and no little bother I introduce them to card and glass salvation, for which they are not remotely thankful. And so to a drink and some talk with the white cat, and to dressing the salad.

Richard Mabey writes to me from Provence where he is 'ambling about'. He says that the Provencals' 'lovely word for this is to *Balade*', and that the countryside is 'going back' rather more flamboyantly than in England. He and Polly are scrumping deserted orchards. Peaches and cherries fall into their thieving hands. It reminds me of mother's rectitude when we pinched apples from the forsaken cottage gardens of our childhood. 'But they don't belong to no one,' we protested. 'No, and they don't belong to you.' Poor apples, poor ivy.

The Transfiguration and Mr Rix's Onions

August 6th

The August butterflies are at their nectar feastings all over the garden, but I dare not name them, for when I have done so in the past, lepidopterists have pounced on me without mercy. Birdsong, butterflies, moths, one can go so wrong. However, white and brown and tortoiseshell butterflies are at this moment all over the place, and a green woodpecker screams ahead of me whenever I go out. And I have preached on the Transfiguration of Jesus nearly a week before the sixth, so what will become of me, heaven only knows. This feast entered the calendar in 1457 to celebrate the victory of the Christians over the Muslims at Belgrade. History makes one despair. Brush it aside. Return to the mountain and that dazzling sight, that eternal and that homely vision, that little praying circle. A brownish-red butterfly beats its wings inside the pane. It beats against my hollowed hands, then soars into the sky.

Boyhood friends complain that I never mention our Suffolk hometown, Sudbury, so I will. I visit a shrine there at least once a month. It is called Waitrose. And I cannot fail to see the three huge wool churches and the statue to Thomas Gainsborough on the Market Hill, and the Croft with its hundred swans, and the Stour with its near-fatal memories (getting half-drowned in it when I was eight), and the farmers' pubs, and the not now quite recognizable faces, for Time insists on re-introductions. As for ghosts, they are now the main population, Canon Hughes on his big black bike, girls who are now old ladies, boys who are old chaps under the grass, music from long-locked organs. Plenty of butterflies in Sudbury, fluttering about the stalls without saying who they are. Ovid would have recognized them as classmates. The country buses come and go, shuddering through the ancient streets, a procession all of its own. I imagine Tom Gainsborough aged eighteen, easel on back, striding to Cornard Wood. I have lunch in the White Horse where his uncle was landlord and watch and watch, which is what writers chiefly do. 'Watch out!' they used to say as the harvest vehicles creaked through the town about this time of the year, squeezing the tarry roads. I cool off in St Gregory's where I worshipped as a young man and heard Canon Hughes thundering the Litany in his Welsh accent, his bald head sparkling with the effort of it. I hear the choir rendering Marbecke and the congregation rising to the occasion. Services, services, 'Shall we see you on Sunday?' What a question! I'm told that people are surprised, or intrigued, to hear that John Updike goes to church every Sunday. He used to write about me in the *New Yorker*, a 'me' I have never quite known, but I never wrote back, of course.

Wormingford is being cut, just fragments of it, not the full harvest. There is a rumbling introit which could only be the trailers in Mr Rix's onions. They are like long boxes with not quite wide enough sides, so the onions leave a nice trail which we are allowed to gather up. It is a kind of onion gleaning. The village school has broken up and some torpor can be expected. Holidays have scattered the congregation to the uttermost parts of the Earth, including Newmarket. There is lull and absence, there is dead-heading and ringing, there is nobody about. But then there rarely is these curious country days when the land is tidy to a T without a worker in sight. Yet, to transpose a glorious acknowledgment, 'It is good, Lord, to be here.'

Home Market-town

August 13th

Botanists still dub certain plants 'mean', never giving them a chance. No species is actually meaner than another when one comes to think about it. This charitable thought arrived on a baking hot day in Sudbury, our shopping town, as I saw the clearance caused by the demolition of a mass of ancient sheds covered with Canadian fleabane, once believed to have arrived in these islands from North America via a stuffed bird. I picked a handsome bit. Like firewood and ragwort it knows how to draw a living veil over dead sites. Then the stroll through the boyhood streets to fill in time before the dentist. There is where Thomas and Margaret Gainsborough lived and from where he walked off one day to paint his friends the Andrews. There is where cousin Peter played cricket and great uncle Ned kept his gig. I rest among old men in the White Horse. They drink a lot of beer and protect their privacy with small talk. Gainsborough's uncle once ran this pub. Just round the corner the house in which Gainsborough Dupart the artist's nephew lived is a pizza parlour. Looking up I can just see the guardian griffins on the parish church where their uncle was rector. They stand sentinal on each pinnacle to keep Satan away. Beyond the plate glass Suffolk chooses to be Midi as the sun reaches new heights. A couple of quotes from the readings for Trinity 15 might sum it up: 'As many as desire to make a fair show in the flesh', and 'And why take ye thought for raiment?' What would Uncle Ned, with his wooden leg and his polished trap and old horse, have thought? Securely buttoned into a thick tobacco-y suit, winter and summer, just the ferrule of his 'timber' leg poking out one end and a curl poking out the other, what existed between was known only to himself and his Maker. The pavements continue to roast with Bank Holiday. 'Give them a day and they take a week,' says one of the old men. For me, this town is a place of my youth and of late in life, so it goes straight from market-day with corn exchange to, on a heatwave like this, an extension of the costas which are now part of these local inhabitants' life, a once unimaginable leisure and prosperity. On the public fountain by the church, put there by a donor concerned with the Victorian work-horses sweltering in the heat, a recent mayor has added a quotation from Dodie Smith's *One Hundred and One Dalmatians*. The author shopped here on market-days, and she is describing Sudbury to her immortal dogs. A chained brass cup, like the Holy Grail, was there when we were children. We swigged from it thirstily, tasting the cold metal, and somehow mysteriously tasting the water in the New Testament.

Visitors to Bottengoms Farm say how quiet it is. 'Not a sound,' they say. When they have disappeared I listen to Delius and begin to hear in the music what I eternally hear outside, or so I believe. Except that one can never tell with composers. My 'silence', so called, amounts to the following noises. The heartbeat of Duncan's grain-dryer, the trackerty-tick, tickerty-track of the Bures train, bees working the balsam, answering pigeons, distant gulls following early ploughing, the waterfall splashing through the centuries, an arthritic ache, a paradisal poplar stirred by a southern wind, one of the loveliest sounds on Earth, a lost plane, falling fruit, a boy calling to a horse, and sometimes – it takes a rest now and then – Little Horkesley church clock. After tea, bell practice will challenge the reticence of this tonal murmur, crash into its clamour. But eventually, when the ropes are hung up, leave it just as it was.

Cutting the Corn

August 15th

Where greengages are concerned there is a moment when one has to beat the wasps and the birds. Just a week late, and ruined fruit will stick to one's hands. Like Polstead cherries, greengages are reckoned a distinctive Suffolk fruit. We gorged on them both as boys. 'If you swallow a wasp, you know what will happen!' What? Warnings without reasons were commonly handed out. To protests about the way we half-washed cos lettuces, we would say, 'But we all have to eat a peck of dirt before we die.' To which mother would respond, 'I daresay, but not all at once.' And now the silky smooth greengages, the prickly ridge-cucumbers. 'And the mixt multitude . . . fell a lusting . . . We remember the cucumbers, and the melons, and the leeks, and the onions, and the garlic . . .' And who does not?

And so to Norwich for Cathedral Camps, the sun burning down and the spire quivering in the heat-haze. The campers, all twenty of them, are hermetically sealed in the Prior's Hall for lunch, and as I do not have the technology to get at them, I wander off to look at their vacated hoovers, mops and pails. Holy Communion from some distant altar falters through the bright arches, tourists read information to each other, nice scrubbed floors mourn minor canons. Then back they come to their toil, beeswaxing ancient stalls already polished by centuries of hands and bottoms, trimming grass edging round the maze and fishing for dust in the under-floor heating. Loose change emerges as from a wishing-well, quite a pile of it, nearly five pounds, they reckon. It is Lucy's seventeenth birthday, so why not spend it on chocolates for her? There is religious consternation. Would those who lost it want it spent thus? Simony crosses their minds. The fret-work iron grills begin to look grim. As someone remarked when I was a teenager, 'Nothing rolls so far as a penny in church.' Has anyone written the history of cathedral clean-ing? I suspect the high angels glimmered through smoky cobwebs, and candle-grease hung down like stalactites.

Harvesting goes on in the village. The buzz of it is con-stant. People remark on the early ploughing, as they always do. It fetches the gulls in from the seaside to make their wintry complaints. But it is full summer all the same, with columbine, ragwort and thistledown, straggling blackberry and swaying hogweed filling the ditches. There are king-fishers by the millrace, the fastest blue on Earth. Cricket is being played with a new emphasis, a fresh glory having been injected by some means or other, myself being subliterate on this score. Yet the ground itself does appear greener, its stripes whiter, its players touched by honour. Children browse along the sweets in the shops, mowers murder scanty lawns. There is a kind of August ennui and lassitude along the main road where the cars keep their paces.

In the cool of St Peter Mancroft at Norwich, I meditate

on the vast, mostly fifteenth-century east window. It is a many-chaptered glass picture-book which is in some respects clearly out of date with some recent doctrines. For example, here are the Apostles gathering for the funeral of the virgin, and the funeral itself, her body corded on a shoulder-held bier, just like those we see on the screen most nights in Iraq. These scenes are as homely as they are divine, and the Assumption is unknown in them. I then make a pilgrimage to the tomb of Sir Thomas Browne.

The Beasts of Denston

August 23rd

The white cat has come in from the cold. 'The cold,' I expostulate, 'but it is only August!' However, she lies on the dresser all day whilst, on the other side of the window, the *Gloire de Dijon* roses fall. Did the deer drive her in? A deer has taken up an heraldic position in the little wood behind the house. He crashes about shyly, and there are furtive glimpses of his scut and his noble head. Should he make a dash for it across the stubble? Or maybe my wood will do for wintering in. But it is only August, I tell him. These animal musings are inspirational when it comes to where to take Graham. Every summer we have to take him to a church which specializes in some wonder or other, preferably in the shape of old glass. At Denston they have collected up, like the crumbs left over from the picnic for the five thousand, the fragments of stained glass left behind by the spoilers and patched them into the east window. Graham will love this colourful scrapbook. And off we drive to Denston, the lanes all scrubbed by yesterday's heavy rain and what remains of the harvest drying-out. We came this way as children to have tea in Mr Hunnable's barn. We call on Monty in his grave at Hawkedon. There he lies, the trim young Battle of Britain airman, under what we noted was a particularly rich piece of wildflower sward. Then on to Denston where the patchwork glass let in exactly the right kind of light for – the animals.

Quite what they were thinking about when they founded this collegiate church just before the Reformation one cannot say, but they filled it with running hares and harts, hounds, birds, lions – even an elephant. They scamper round the clerestory and snooze on the stalls and benches. A crane lurks below one of the misericords. As a boy, Denston reminded me of a toy Noah's ark crammed with cut-out wooden animals, except that these had a static quality when one lifted the lid, whereas on Judgement Day at Denston, when God lifted the roof, for this is what I imagined would happen, the carved creatures were lively enough to leap out into Suffolk, leaving humanity to its fate.

Animals are one way of entering the medieval mind. Men and beasts were hugger-mugger then, just as they were during the Nativity, sharing the shelter and the load. Mr Hunnable's ancestors would have heard them in the thatch, behind the wall, on the hearth, restless, warm, companionable, never far away. Their religion was crowded with creatures – at this moment ours is remembering the trouble Jonah had with his whale – and, naturally, they came into church. In fact more birds, mammals and insects than we would now care to think about took up permanent residence in church, and even today bats in the belfry are honoured guests. Who honoured St Nicholas, Denston, with a bestiary? Who proposed hares and harts and cranes instead of angels? Who brought the delight of outdoors indoors? When the iconoclasts arrived they chipped off the heads of the saints but left all the animals to play around as they had done since the Wars of the Roses. Or to slumber on the pews. Their heads patted by centuries of listeners.

Medieval creatures had their own *Who's Who*. A marvellous one is the twelfth-century *Book of Beasts*, translated by T. H. White.

The Trouble with Artists

September 12th

It is the Royal British Legion Flower Show in the village hall again. Almost everything is again. 'The committee has power to settle any matter.' Ian and I judge the school paintings. They are wild. Footballers find their way through orange seas, mum and dad attack each other on scarlet tennis courts, creatures get out of the way. But there is, again, the inevitable masterpiece. A pair of stripey arms clasps a rugby ball, the two ovoid shapes revealing the artist's sense of design. Exhibitors plant runner-beans, apples and roses on the kitchen-paper beds which stretch the length of the room. They include those with a past, Donald (Kohima), Harold (the Atlantic Convoy), Gordon (El Alamein). The latter is being bossed about by the lady judge whose verdict is final. She feeds him with crumbs from Victorian sponges, biscuits, loaves and watches his face. Marmalade, jams, homemade wines touch his lips. And hers. They mumble and collude. Cups glimmer on the platform. The raffle man does a good trade. Out of the corner of my eye I watch my Victoria plums getting a First and my photos of A Winter Scene getting the elbow. Opposite, a large field-map of our village shines on the wall – not that it would get you any- where these days, for here spreads a foreign country. Please can you tell me the way to Commollicus, to Dods Hole, to Great Fridgetts. Am I right for Linky Field? When all is judged, Donald and I have a pint in the Crown for there is nothing more to be done other than give the prizes. There is a kind of wistfulness, the pleasant regret which for me lurks in Jeremiah's 'The harvest is past, and the summer is ended, and we are not saved.'

Isaiah, his fellow poet-prophet, once found himself worried about artists' licence, not to mention art altogether. 'Show me the artisan who isn't tempted to go beyond his brief and become an artist,' he says. They are to build the Temple, and the blacksmith and the carpenter will carry the skills of their trades into idolatry if they are not watched, circumscribed, held back. There must be no arts and crafts movement in the Temple. His warnings, needless to add, were of no avail. The Temple rose, a building strongly constructed and gloriously adorned. And Isaiah's fears about the blacksmith and the carpenter not being able to hold back from creating an image of God were briefly quelled. It was the carpenter who worried him most. When the blacksmith returned home, tired after a day at the forge, he was most likely to drop-off after supper as he sat by the hearth, and no harm done. But the carpenter! This was quite another story. The prophet muses upon what led a craftsman into the dangerous business of art. He begins at the beginning. There is the wildwood, then the planted wood – 'He planteth an ash' – and after the carpenter has done his work for the day there is firewood to cook his meal and to keep him warm. Not dozing, very much alive as artists tend to be, he sees a nice bit of wood lying by his feet and he begins to whittle it with his knife. Goodness knows how many 'father's chairs' there are whose right arms show signs of whittling as toys and pegs and curiously imaginative objects were idly fashioned of an evening. Watch out! says Isaiah. An honest tradesman is becoming an artist.

The carpenter should be resting after doing the work which was required of him. But no. He whittles away and 'maketh a god, his graven image'. But the carpenter, and eventually the blacksmith, go on 'whittling', and, hey presto, Michelangelo's *David* and Gormley's *Angel of the North*, and the image-filled church. So Isaiah was right.

William Hazlitt on Jesus Christ

September 17th

How simple it is to translate oneself, to change one's sky, or in my case trees. Three hours ago I was under my oaks, rained down on by acorns, now I am under the still leaves of a London square, waiting for the lecture to begin. Behind me is Conway Hall, the home of the South Place Ethical Society, in front of me are two lovers who have to brace themselves together if they are not to fall over, so urgent is their engagement. A hundred pigeons doze at our feet, and the sweet, already faintly rotting smell of the September air shifts lazily around us. The lecture audience creeps warily over the grass, careful not to be too late or too early. It is Saturday afternoon, when the West End is neither at work nor at play. The lovers topple apart, the birds fly up, and I enter the hall. It is packed. How did all these people get in without my noticing? A father's advice to his son, 'To thine own self be true', is painted above the platform and the room settles to further rational thinking, for this is the inaugural lecture of the Hazlitt Society, of which I am a vice-president, and we are to listen to A. C. Grayling on 'Hazlitt: The Independent Mind'.

Everyone should read William Hazlitt, especially at this moment. When I recommend him to all and sundry, they recollect, if they are aged, 'doing' him for school cert, or if they are youthful, that he was an essayist, and who reads essays now? Well, those who read certain journalists, might be the reply, although these latter should top up both their thinking and their style with Hazlitt and his mentor Montaigne. Once begun on an Hazlitt essay, it becomes irresistible. It hurries the eye along, it clears the head, it creates new courage, it brightens life. Even when he is hating – he prided himself on being a good hater – he is never hateful. And when he is loving – well! Brought up a Unitarian, detesting, like William Blake, the Church of England, and in no way 'religious', he once gave a lecture entitled 'Jesus Christ' which swept aside much of the sermonizings of his age. It began:

> There is something in the character of Christ (leaving religious faith quite out the question) of more sweetness and majesty, and more likely to work a change in the mind of man, by the contemplation of its idea alone, than any to be found in history, whether actual

or feigned. This character is of a sublime humanity,
such as was never seen on earth before or since. This
shone manifestly both in his words and actions . . .
His religion was the religion of the heart . . . His whole
life and being were imbued, steeped in this word
charity: it was the spring, the well-head from which
every thought and feeling gushed into act . . . He was
the first true teacher of morality; for he alone con-
ceived the idea of pure humanity . . . He taught the
love of good for the sake of good . . . In the Christian
religion we perceive a softness coming over the heart
of a nation.

This, of course, was his radical perception of the gospel in
all its freshness and infancy, and not that taught by ortho-
doxy. He was greatly accepting of his father's faith as he
watched the old Unitarian minister, isolated in the countryside (when, like his son, he would much rather have been
in the thick of things in the city), half-blind, poring over
the Bible days on end, finding 'neither poetry nor philos-
ophy' but only 'the sacred name JEHOVAH pressed down
by weight of style, worn to the last fading thinness of the
understanding.

Insect Thinking

September 20th

Settling below the tomatoes on the east wall, I experience the usual futility of reading when the sun glitters through leaves and time itself takes a break. I might have sunk into torpor had it not been for the dragonfly on my knee. Gradually, landing and taking off several times, it became an object for meditation. It flew a few yards, then walked on bare skin with an adventurous uncertainty like a man on the moon. I could see cyclamen through its translucent wings. Invisible behind a hedge, someone set up a mighty clanging like a wild call to arms as the horses' water-trough was mended, and I turned a page, but still the dragonfly did not alter its course of brief flights and short stays. I assumed it was a Darter, being at that September moment deficient in Odonata knowledge and not liking to deprive it of its living pad as I searched for a natural history book. And thus we continued for an hour or more, the motionless man and the sensational insect, the banging in the meadow and the delectable autumn day.

Later, I read my favourite insect-contemplation essay, 'The Death of the Moth' by Virginia Woolf: 'It was a pleasant morning, mid-September, mild, benignant, yet with a keener breath than that of the summer months . . . Such vigour came rolling in from the fields [when] the same

energy which inspired the rooks, the ploughmen, the horses
... sent the moth fluttering from side to side of his square
of the window-pane.' She should have opened the window
and let it out, but she went on working and the moth danced
his way to death. Soon she would fill her pockets with stones
and walk to the river. The Kentish poet Sidney Keyes wrote
her Elery.

> Unfortunate lady, where white crowfoot binds
> Unheeded garlands starred with crumpled flowers,
> Lie low, sleep well, safe from the rabid winds
> Of war and argument, our hierarchies and powers.

The Old Testament writers had a sharp eye for insects, as
one would expect in the Middle East. Samson's riddle about
the bees hiving in a dead lion is delightful. Tate and Lyle
printed the answer, 'Out of the strong came forth sweetness',
on their treacle tins. The Lord hisses up flies and bees and
young David calls poor old Saul a flea. Judges spin webs as
wiley snares, and enemies such as the Amorites chase one
as bees do. But on the whole, Bible insects are a plague and
ages would pass before a country clergyman would observe
dispassionately, 'After the servants are gone to bed, the
kitchen hearth swarms with minute crickets not so large as
fleas, which must have been lately hatched. So that these
domestic creatures, cherished by the influence of a constant
large fire, regard not the season of their year, but produce
their young at a time when their congeners are either dead,

or laid up for the winter, to pass away the uncomfortable months in the profoundest slumbers . . .' Why did Virginia Woolf not open the window, then her moth would have lived? Why am I sitting here in the faintly rotting autumn garden long past elevenses so that a dragonfly can do whatever it is that dragonflies do on a nice quiet leg? Its pond shimmers through the nettles but it is me it is eyeing with all its eyes.

The Absent God

September 26th

Taking the service, I am frequently conscious of saying prayers without praying, of directing and not worshipping. Prayer will not put up with this sort of thing for long and, like cheerfulness, will break in. There is a kind of time struggle between the strict demands of liturgy and what the congregation might tolerantly conceive as my fancifulness, my hopelessly impractical fate as a writer. I supplement Matins and Evensong prayers with some now fairly ancient compositions of my own, and now and then with a marvellous discovery from long ago, although not with the prayer which Venkayya, the first outcaste convert to the Church of South India, offered every day for three years, 'O great God, who art thou? Where art thou? Show thyself to me.' The poet-priest R. S. Thomas every now and then had to ask the same question. Instead I might quote from *The Cloud of Unknowing* c. 1350, 'Look on cheerfully and tell your Lord, either aloud or in your heart, "What I am, Lord, I offer you, for it is yourself." And keep in mind, simply, plainly, and unashamedly, that you are as you are, and that there is no need to inquire more closely.' Prayer is spring-water compared with the turgid ocean of theology. It bubbles up during the minute monthly Evensong in St Andrew's where the churchwardens, Barry, John, the Colonel and his wife face one another in the chancel, and the tower clock clunks towards seven, the summer presses in at the door and we are clearly refreshed by it, myself particularly, at this service having gone only through its motions. Although Christ drew a distinction between public worship and private prayer – 'Enter into thy closet' – I always feel that he would have loved the Church's compromise of private prayer in a public building. We count communicants but cannot count the prayerful, those workers who drop in on God during the lunch hour, those who, Pevsner in hand, come to look and stay to pray. As Queen Victoria told John Brown after his father's funeral, 'The use of the Church was that it made one think of what one would not otherwise think of.' Exactly.

I am picking her plums, pailsful of them. They dangle in glossy ropes to the grass and are nearly as delicious to touch as to eat. They are stoned and packed away in the freezer, also gobbled raw. Wasps feed at my feet. Kitty elevates herself above this gorging in the walnut tree. Warm showers fall heavily and we are both drenched. This is when the woodland birds turn up the sound. Cats are supposed to hate getting wet but this one purrs it out, as indeed do I, for the harvesting of fruit for the bare days to come is among the pleasures of September. I must feed to the ramblers what cannot be stored or gorged, for Victorias have no shelf life. At night, owls cry across the valley. Muntjacs and foxes bark. It is wild out there. And briefly smelly, for the fields have been manured just in time for the rain to splash it in.

I sit near the front door re-reading Matthew Arnold, travelling with him to Cornwall, Brittany, Dover Beach, Calaise Sands, the Alps, Paris, Hyde Park, Etna, to the bedside of *The Sick King in Bokhara*, the rich sadness invading my garden, the tiny handwritten notes which Canon Gerald Rendall made still instructive. He purchased this beautiful edition in 1859. Sheltering in a French church, Arnold listens to 'The rustle of the eternal rain of love'.

A Late Harvest

September 30th

B y the moss rose, a baby hare scarcely big enough to warrant the name leveret trembles. It seems unconscious of my presence and is immobile. Transparent ears through which the morning shines. The white cat approaches, so what to do? A single clap of my hands sends the leveret to safety and the cat to sulks. It is my Cowper good deed for the day. The air is still dusty from yesterday's harvesting. There is a wheat powdering of oak and ash. The ponds are a delicate grey but the shorn field, an enormous one, is as gold as you can get. Also – car-bound churchwardens rejoice and be glad – my track has received its annual pre-harvest hair-cut, and never a better one. 'Track!' it protests, 'look at me. I am a Saxon highway! Mr Sycamore and Farmer Tom Bradshaw have had their way with me.' Tom has even gone so far as to reply to the usual harvesting groans, in his village newsletter, with 'If you see the combine going to the field please take the opportunity to shut all your windows and take your washing off the line.' Down by St Andrew's, the onion wagons scrape past worshippers' cars with just an inch to spare. Why people have to go to church just when the harvest tackle takes to the lanes beats the drivers. The bells, which once heard the excited shouts of 'They're cutting at Garnons!' now ignore the whole business. Turning my John Clare lectures into a book, I don't have to wonder what happened in his day. For there it is, every exhausting moment of it, every custom, every ritual joy and pain. And I can just see a Helpston farmer apologising for the inconvenience. Those who brought the harvest home would have swayed across their own thresholds at moonlit midnight, scratched to bits, and a little drunk, as they deserved to be.

Upon the waggon now, with eager bound,
The luster picker whirls the rustling sheaves;
Or, resting ponderous creaking fork aground,
Boastful at once whole shocks of barley heaves:
The loading boy revengeful inly grieves
To find his unmatched strength and power decay;
The barley horn his garments interweaves;
Smarting and sweating 'neath the sultry day,
With muttering curses stung, he mauls the heaps away.

Houses are taking a long time to sell, they say. The agents'
signboards wave rather desperately from trim hedges for
months on end. Yet those searching for something of character, as they call it, still have to search wide and hard. Having
never bought a house it is all a mystery to me. It is clear
that there are folk who just like a nice change and who
move the mortgage on. The young are offered jobs they can't
refuse, and off they go, like birds to a better bush, like Mark
and his wife, who have only just got the curtains up and the
garden right. But there it is. Walking to the post office, I bid
good-day to the latest strangers. But my hornets return time
and time again to delight me and terrify the guests. One is
reading my dictionary at this moment, buzzing across the
page like a tiny tractor. If it could turn the page it would
see that it is our largest wasp, a tawny yellow social wasp
more than an inch long, which uses its fearsome sting on
man only if attacked. 'Wasp,' I say, 'I am a man of peace.'

Discoed Diaries

October 1st

To where I still want to call Radnorshire. An annual obligation eventually makes one a local of sorts, and here are the by now dear familiar faces, though their names still need a bit of remembering. It is the Michaelmas Wakes at Discoed and I am to talk about Angels and Diarists, although not at the same time. Jackdaws twizzle on the weathervane, cats stroll on Offa's Dyke, Dilwyn hurries in and out of church with music stands, beautiful soup wafts from somewhere near the font, the rector escapes from rehearsing *Princess Ida* to read Francis Kilvert for me – that fearsome entry describing the dream of his killing of his rector with a pickaxe and waking up to hear the clock striking morning – and other Discoedians reading from the *Journals* of Dorothy Wordsworth, Cornelius Stovin, Queen Victoria, Lady Eleanor Butler . . . Outside a great yew which measured its life in millennia darkened for the latest owls. 'What do you think,' Edward told me, 'the other day I looked out and saw a ring of Pagans standing around it!'

The following day we dash into Presteigne – 'the border meadow of the priests' – to fetch food and I have to be hauled from a marvellous muddle of a shop – 'All books 50p' – where I just have time to purchase *Why Birds Sing* by Jacques Delamain (1928), a lovely treasure which I might give to Richard Mabey. Writing to the friend who had, for three terrible years, fought alongside him on the Western Front, Delamain says that he has been reading Gilbert White and Lord Grey and noting that

> The Anglo-Saxon race, and in a more general fashion, the Protestant races, are infinitely more interested in all this winged world than the Catholic Latins. One might, in the manner of Michelet, comment extensively upon this. For Catholicism, nature always remains more or less the enemy. The mystic Catholic lives turned in upon himself, attentive only to his most profound interior reality. God is in him; it is in himself that he seeks Him and tries to grasp Him. A mystic like Saint Francis of Assisi, so great a friend of the beasts and of our inferior brethren, is only an exception to the rule. Therefore, I am not surprised that he should be about the only one among the saints to have captivated the Protestant mind . . .

So now we know why little song-birds, those which we protect and adore for their music, are shot, plucked and made a mouthful of in France and Italy.

The first day of October in Wales. The borders lie in a subdued light which turns the hills a tawny brown. The clouds ride low and sheep move in little surges over the autumn grass. When we drive to friends who live above a thousand feet we can see the Malvern Hills like a pink smudge in the ultimate distance. Here is Credenhill where Thomas Traherne wrote his *Centuries*. Below his church are the SAS barracks and the tree-lined road to Hereford. 'When I came into the Country, and being seated among silent trees, had all my Time in my own Hands, I resolved to spend it all, whatever it cost me, in Search of Happiness, and to Satiate that burning thirst which Nature had en-kindled in me from youth.' When I come into Wales, I tell my poet friend Edward, I cannot stop looking, listening. Or talking, if it comes to that, for we have much in common. Traherne's was such a short life. Ours have been long, if no more than the dropping of a needle to the Discoed yew. But there it is, our time here, our timelessness elsewhere.

Luke and His Little Summer

October 18th

Fetching the morning milk at midnight from the top of the track, I watch the Stansted planes weaving silently in and out of the Plough every thirty seconds. A vast canopy of stars hangs over the shedding trees. My resident owl crashes from the hazels. The October air is warm, damp and lulling. The Plough reminds me of John Constable making sketches further along the river for a picture he would call 'Landscape-Noon' until his friend John Fisher enquired, 'How thrives the hay wain?' There are actually two hay carts in this painting, an empty one in the river and a dizzily piled one in the distance where a dozen men are scything the water-meadow. Willy Lott's bedroom window is wide and a honeysuckle climbs toward it. During their midnight hour these Stour folk would have picked out, not the Plough, but Charles's Wain. Pictures, stars, plans, we ourselves, often answer to two names. My windows open, I go to bed in the half-dark so as not to invite hornets. There are increasing animal cries in the valley and the occasional swish of ash leaves on the sill. 'Multitudes, multitudes in the valley of decision,' wrote Joel, 'for the day of the Lord is near in the valley of decision . . . the stars shall withdraw their shining.' The fragmented beauty of the language which runs through one's head at bedtime.

Luke and his little summer is in sight. I plant bulbs. Their depth in the earth has to be twice their size. The white cat lies full length on the ancient wall. Any human activity increases her languor. She purrs thunderously, blinking me out when I lift my gaze in her direction. Her indoor perch is now in the study and when she stretches various master-pieces rain down. 'It won't do,' I tell her. She regards me goldenly from some feline bliss.

To Birmingham Cathedral to preach at a service to cele-brate the ministry of older people. It is part of the diocesan centenary celebration. Both the cathedral and the city centre amaze me – and the multi-racial people. I feel I want to make the rest of the country go there to see what has hap-pened to Birmingham, previously a place as unknown to me as Timbuktu, a festoon in my head of spaghetti roads, and now quite wonderful. St Philip's is enchanting, a classical Georgian temple with flaming Burne-Jones windows, and filled to the brim with aged saints. Except for the archbishop, the dean, the canons, the musicians (lads) every seat is taken by what the Church of England constantly and crudely calls 'an elderly congregation'. My sermon is about such ageism, about Anna and Simeon, about Time and ourselves, and we sing Tim Dudley-Smith's 'Lord, for the years your love has kept and guided' and the archbishop reads from Evelyn Underhill, and I remember that it is the retired who do half the church work in this country, never taking a penny for it. Much of this extraordinary event is due to the decidely un-Trollopian master of a Tudor charity, James Woodward. In the vestry the archbishop talks to me briefly about York and I wish him all happiness. He blesses me. Lunch – whitebait – in a glass restaurant. Then the Euston train and phones going off in all directions, and leafy Warwickshire living up to its name, and the rain snaking down the carriage windows, and the lights going on all over Watford.

Back at Bottengoms I pick a few tomatoes for dinner and riffle through the post. A soaking cat dries off on my best suit and earthquakes roar away on the radio, and the hymns for Matins must be found.

In Vikram Seth's House

October 18th

To Bemerton once again. The ticket collector has to unlock the carriage window to let a final burst of summer in. The trackside hills turn from loam to chalk. Judy Rees meets me at Salisbury station and soon we are in Bemerton church, opening the door which George Herbert opened, listening to the bell which he heard, taking the silver cup which he held. A butterfly beats against the high window. I read the Lesson, the favourite one in which Paul is telling Timothy to pick up Mark, the cloak which he left at Troas, his books – especially 'my notebooks', and in which he complains, 'Only Luke is with me.' Only Luke! Well. I give Herbert's cup to the communicants. It would have gone from hand to hand as the poet released it to earl and ploughman alike, this Tudor drinking vessel with its steep sides and flowering rim, and each would have been humbled and elevated, as the case might be. Canon Rees and myself tread to and fro over the sacred dust.

After this, another table is laid on which to sign my book *George Herbert at Bemerton* and have tea. The sun goes in abruptly and it turns cold. It is my first glimpse of the book in which Vikram Seth has written a Foreword. He can't be here because he is signing a book, *Two Lives*, abroad. Terry

Pratchett is signing his new book in Salisbury, they say. When did all this authorial signing start? Soon I am standing in Herbert's bedroom across the busy road, the same one in which he rose from his deathbed to sing a hymn from the window, and then entrusted a fat bundle of poems to his old schoolfriend Nicholas Ferrar. 'Burn them if they are no good.' But they went swiftly to Little Gidding and then to the best Cambridge printer. Writers instantly know the worth of writings. Luke put his books into the safe hands of the mysterious Theophilus, a Greek friend who sounds like a publisher. I stare out of Herbert's bedroom window into his garden. The bare floorboards are wide, like those at home, and look like elm. Elm for floors – and coffins. And for bookshelves, of course. I can see the River Nadder glinting below Vikram's lawn and acres of water meadows beyond. Like St Paul, Herbert wrote,

> I will complain, yet praise,
> I will bewail, approve;
> And all my sowre-sweet days
> I will lament, and love.

They put his coffin under the church floor on Quinquagesima Sunday, the epistle for which has St Paul looking through a glass darkly and thinking about tongues ceasing. The apostle would not have known about stained glass, the pictures capturing the eye until it looks further and goes beyond the glass surface and 'then the heav'n espie'. Passing

from room to room in Herbert's–Vikram's airy house, I
imagine music.

All Souls

October 31st

October, a time of sumptuous colour, singing wind and
scuttling creatures in East Anglia. Leaves not only fall
but can be heard being thrown about by nutters, rabbits
and dogs. Even the children manage a little of the old kick-
rustling between the car and the classroom. My dozen oaks
rattle down acorns, dead wood and more or less unmulch-
able leaves by the million. Let it all lie until there is bareness
above and crunch below. It occurs to me that I probably
possess rights of pannage with all this mast descending on
my grass every autumn, all these 'eykornes' (Saxon), all this
rich swine food. Mast was a kind of wood salad consisting
of, not only oak fallings, but bark, souring grass below trees,
fungi, truffles and whatever lay on the October ground
generally. Alas, the pigs now live in pigtown and far from
this woody spread. They squelch in front of hooped concrete
dwellings, sometimes lifting their snouts maybe to catch a
whiff of their forest restaurants on the breeze. Chronic
mowers on Saturday afternoon walks cast a worried eye
on my lawn, the one which catches the mast. They shake

their heads and wonder if the garden is becoming too much for me.

At the back of the church they are filling up the list of the dead. It is rather like a new address-book. Who should be left on from last time, who added. All Saints for All Souls. When the roll is called up yonder, I'll be there. What passings there have been, what seats vacated. It is a wonder that we can continue. Dear familiar faces and unknown faces fade in and out on the biroed list. A tiny pause between each life, each death. The living kneel as I read them out, musing on Judgement Day or a recent funeral, on resurrection or poor old Tom having to listen to all this when the wreaths still lie on his wife's grave, flowers which, given a chance, might well go to mast.

Young Richard Rolle died on Michaelmas Day, 1349, when there was no option to say yes to Death as it meant yes to Life. So he wrote,

> Death, why do you delay? Why are you so slow in coming to me, a man alive but mortal? Why do you not catch hold of him who is longing for you? Who can possibly assess that sweetness which brings an end to all sighing, a beginning to all blessedness, the gate to a desired, unfailing joy? . . . If you come I will be safe . . . For this same poor man is taken after death to the place where angels sing, because he has been cleansed and blessed, and now lives in the Spirit's music. He, who all his life has based his meditation on that lovely Name, will die surrounded by marvellous melody.

Most of us live for ages now and the longer we live, the more we would live. I add my parents' names to the All Souls' list although I will be the only one in church who can see their faces. In Thomas Hardy the quick hung around the churchyard on All Souls to see who would go the following year, treading the wet turf and mumbling, 'Man that is born of woman . . .' mortality then being a major form of village entertainment. He took a dramatic Stanley Spenserish view of it all, though minus the joy. The hosts of heaven greet Richard Rolle with hymns and 'take him with honour to the court of the Emperor Eternal . . . Love brought him to this state.' Love, when one comes to think it, has brought us to where we are.

Widermund's Ford

November 4th

November and the garden seat covered with books and coffee cups – and cat. Skimpy yellow clouds sail on high. Ash leaves like withered hands caress us as they tumble into wet grass. There is a nice whiff of rot. I stroll to the river to make my autumn observance and the dace – I think – flash under the bridge. The iron rail is hot and the mill-pool offers a swim. In my head global warming fights with bliss. I think of Widermund the Saxon setting out the sarsons which the plough has turned up to make stepping-stones in the ford so that people could cross the Stour from one kingdom to another without wetting their feet. Widermund's ford, due to much ancestral garbling, became Wormingford – the Dragon's ford. In vain do I teach etymology to the neighbours – 'ety-what?' In vain do I wonder that boys are not christened Widermund – instead of Charlie, say. Widermund's face doesn't appear in the stained glass but the Dragon's does as he munches a virgin. Her snowy bare legs dangle from his jaw and so concentrating is he on his dinner that he fails to see George. A new altar has been set beneath this alarming scene.

Theologically, dragons are only afraid of the Panther, not George. In his *Book of Beasts* T. H. White says, 'What Solomon pointed out about Christ is symbolized by the panther being an animal of so many colours that by the wisdom of God the Father he is the Apprehensible Spirit, the Only Wise, the Manifold, the True, the Sweet, the Suitable, the Clement, the Constant, the Established, the Untroubled, the Omnipotent, the All-Seeing. And because it is a beautiful animal, the Lord God says of Christ: "He is beautiful in form among the sons of men".' But no panthers in the north aisle and, a mile or two upstream, above the north door of Wiston church, it is a dragon that gloats over those whose fate it is to be buried 'on the dog' (bestiaries tend to go rather wild and have never heard of David Attenborough). 'On the dog' means the north churchyard, an unhallowed spot crammed with unmarried mothers, unbaptized babies, suicides and paupers. Dragon food. Ours at Wormingford contains some very grand tombs, including those of John Constable's uncles who ran the mill by Widermund's ford and whose chief dragon was the collapse of agriculture after the Napoleonic wars.

I miss filling up my Wild Flower Society Register but having done so a dozen times there seems no point in writing, 'Wild Teasel, *Dipsacus fullonum*, Garnon's field bank' for the thirteenth time. For there it may have been since Widermund scratched himself on it. But one feels guilty when one ceases to take note of plants. Those who did so incurred the wrath of John Clare. He was a rural looker. Nothing growing, flying, running, swimming, taking to its bed in autumn escaped his eye, and he would lash out at villagers who stumped to and fro in Helpston, apparently not seeing a thing. But they and he both saw ghosts, of course. You might miss *Dipsacus fullonum* but you would never miss a ghost. The closest he gets to dragons is a crocodile which recognizes 'the Ichneumon (mongoose) as its destroyer'. Yet all the mongoose wanted from the crocodile was its eggs. Clare bridges all the science and mythology of the English countryside in his poetry. We see where we came from – and where we are going. His river was the Nene. It glitters and frowns in his work, sucks at the fenny ground, fills sluices, widens into little paradises.

St Martin's Day in Colchester

November 11th

St Martin's little summer, so make the most of it. This I
tell myself, finding a hood to protect my ears from its
underlying chill and wellingtons to splosh through the tractor ruts. Martin was an army officer who gave half his cloak
to a naked man, which one hopes was adequate. His feast
is actually on Remembrance Day, a complex coincidence as
he resigned his commission in order to be in a quite different
regiment – 'I am Christ's soldier; I am not allowed to fight',
thus becoming a prototype of World War One's and Two's
conscientious objection. Like these objectors, he was
accused of cowardice, but after having offered to stand un-
armed between the lines he was given an honourable dis-
charge and eventually went off to join St Hilary, one of the
first people to teach the gospel by the use of metrical hymns
– and to be a married bishop. I imagine the pair of them
wonderworking in late sunshine, the ex-officer and tough
but good-natured theologian, one who gave his name to a
university term, the other who would have approved of
General Booth. I often sit in St Martin's churchyard in
Colchester, my shopping on a nice flat tomb, with the chest-
nut-tree leaves whirling around and the blunt tower – it was
shot off by General Fairfax's guns during the Civil War –
casting a jagged shadow. Aldermen and their ladies lie

around under the rank grass. A few doors down is the steep house in which Jane Taylor wrote 'Twinkle, twinkle, little star' and her sister Anne wrote,

> Lazy sheep, pray tell me why
> In the pleasant fields you lie,
> Eating grass, and daisies white,
> From the morning till the night?
> Every thing can something do,
> But what kind of use are you?

There are further verses which take the edge off this harsh question. And then further down still, is the corner house in which Defoe began *Moll Flanders* which is strictly for grown-ups. These St Martin's folk, my having known them all my life, are part of my local family. Young soldiers clatter by them of an evening en-route to pubs and clubs with never a salute for the saint, whilst overhead, dulled by the street lights, it is twinkle, twinkle, little planes.

On the eve of St Martin I pack it in, as they say. Work. His sun hits the sill where the cat sprawls, hits the desk too. So I walk out of the study into autumn gold, taking the unmade lane to the new reservoir where ducks, geese and gulls are creating a bird regatta. The water is sky-blue, the summer grass blonde, the wind is in the west. Oaks, probably the crop planted after all the others had been used up for Nelson's ships, are tinged with their annual mortality and are brown shadows of their June selves. The most recent ones, aged about twenty, have burst their rabbit guards like

Samson bursting his chains, and stand clear of protection. Not a soul about. Vapour trails are scrawled all over what the Taylor girls would have called heaven. I realize I'm a new man, and all due to walking a couple of miles across the fields. And why go in again – ever? Martin, after all, is perpetually 'in the fields' in London. He was ever journeying by land and water, by donkey-back, by foot, and his sunshine.

Christ the King

November 26th

The white cat and I have one thing in common – we are immediate wakers. None of that dozy inbetween business for us, we are either dead to the world or suddenly alive in it. Who are we when we sleep? I watch David Beckham sleeping in the National Portrait Gallery, and the commuting girl asleep on the train. How vulnerable they are. I imagine Himmler asleep, his rimless glasses on the bedside table, tomorrow's orders by their side. I creep in to kiss the sleeping child goodnight. But now it is dark morning and black trees, and the cat ordering breakfast pronto. And a page on my desk saying, 'To be continued.' I tell the cat, 'It is vain for you to rise up early, to sit up late, to eat the bread of sorrows, for so he giveth his beloved sleep.' And what a gift. But all she hears is the word 'eat'. A nice slow light heralds Christ the King. Pius XI inaugurated this now popular observance for the last Sunday in November in 1925, perhaps after reading in Revelation, 'The kingdoms of this world are become the kingdoms of our Lord and of his Christ.' And old Cowley Father once told me, 'When I was young it was all Christ the King but now it is all Christ the Servant, and I have to get used to it.' This was before the hymn obligingly healed the rift. The new morning is not unlike my and the cat's swift awakenings, inky one minute, clear as daylight the next. Having gobbled-up the bread of sorrows, aka Whiskas, she returns to oblivion, and I tap out a sentence or two, just to show willing.

Radio Three is playing something by Beethoven's father Johann. I think of the little Elector listening to it as he plays Tric-trac with his ladies. Johann, they said, taught his son nothing but music, and that quite savagely in order to make him a wage-earner at six. The burgomaster, passing the house, glimpsed the tiny Ludwig, or Louis as they called him then, standing in front of the clavier and weeping. Having just come to the last page of Vikram Seth's marvellous novel *An Equal Music* I too could weep. No more chapters, no more words, just the back cover, just the now redundant bookmarker. All done. My sister said that she read it through a second time, not able to leave these lovers and their quartet, their London and Rochdale and Venice. But I must have a space in my head for them to play Bach in for a long time to come. I haven't been so overwhelmed by a novel about musicians since, in my teens, I read Henry Handel Richardson's *Maurice Guest*. Vikram Seth took his title from John Donne's prayer – the one I always say at village funerals, 'And into that gate they shall enter, and in that house they shall dwell, where there shall be no cloud nor sun, no darkness nor dazzling, but one equal light, no noise nor silence, but an equal music, no fears nor hopes, but one equal possession, no foes nor friends, but one equal communion and identity, no ends nor beginnings, but one equal eternity.'

I clear the breakfast things and shake the cloth over the sodden grass. After a cautious five minutes, two wrens appear, small and trembling. Perfect creatures. They eat in a kind of terror. A speck of apple, a toast crumb, then a wary flight to a furry leaf, and this over and over again. The weather contradicts the forecast and is damp and moody. Radio Three plays on but, like the Elector, I am often not hearing it, this equal music, and am ashamed. I am thinking what to say about King Jesus and should I plant more bulbs.

The Dark Day

November 29th

I walk to Advent Matins in a thin cold drizzle. Supermarket shoppers zip past. I can hear our bells getting into their stride. How pleased widow Sturdy would have been to know that the bell she created in her foundry was in good ringing order all these centuries later. The footballers are not yet in their stride. Damp, noisy and listless, they trot up and down to keep warm. Their dogs gaze from car windows telling each other, 'More fool they!' In church, strangers take up an entire pew. Well! I light the Advent candle, say the Advent words, sing the Advent tunes;:

> Ring, bells, ring, ring, ring!
> Sing, choirs, sing, sing, sing!

And there, long ago, is dear Mr Pratt Green waiting for me at Norwich Station.

> Long ago, prophets knew
> Christ would come, born a Jew.

What a dark day it is. Black shiny lanes, lightless furrows, horses in their gloomy blankets, shadows tramping home with the Sunday papers, but my little white cat illuminating the ebony piano, having knocked all the photos down. Shall we light a fire? Shall we read all afternoon? Shall we garden? Shall we heck! as Gordon would say. I listen to Bach's

Goldberg Variations, or some of them, and although it would seem impossible the day grows darker without it actually falling into night. Returning via the orchard I had noticed the reluctance of the leaves to reach the ground. More sticks than foliage had been shaken out of the oaks, and the walnut was deathly in its sodden unshed growth. There were lots of wrens, tiny feathery balls with tails cocked and, fast as lightning, having supper. The vast ivy on the ancient pear rustled with inmates and had become a bird town. Everywhere, inner Advent light and outer darkness.

Roger Deakin arrives and we discuss wood. Wood as a material, ours being a part of the country which lacks stone. We have flint, of course, flinty fields, flint mines even, but little that one could call stone. So we have done what we could with wood. East Anglia is for wood architects, wood artists, wood saints, woodland poets and wood crafts. Looking around at the uses we have put it to you would think that there would not be a tree standing – but we remain heavily wooded. The dark day polishes the beams of Bottengoms, showing off the adze marks. How many trees were chopped down to make this small farmhouse? Have a guess. It is Tudor Ikea plus straw stuffing, all the beams slotted into place for eternity, and the brick floors scrubbed hollow. Visitors coming to it at nightfall, such as the poor vicar, are apt to wander around in a botanical version of outer darkness, shocked by startled pheasants going off like rockets. Or lacerated by yuccas. I comfort them. Are they not experiencing the genuine one hundred per cent authentic rural November teatime? They should praise God for it.

Sparks thread their way overhead. Each contains hundreds of folk on their way to New York, Rome, Moscow, those by the windows staring down at my spark.

The Quince Tree

December 3rd

I find myself relishing the failing light, the brief afternoons, the cross birds waiting for me to pack up, chiffchaffs and pheasants mostly, joining in noisy protest as I continue to garden when, at 4 p.m., every decent December creature should be in bed. The sun sets like a watery egg and the top field becomes a black wall. But still I clear the orchard. At the moment it is the desperate task of sawing dead wood from the ancient Portugal quince and I feel like one of the surgeons in Nelson's navy – 'Bite the bullet, my lad. You'll be better off without it.' Off comes a vast limb. Half the quince flourishes, half has gone wherever quinces go when they are past bearing. But the tree has a history parallel with my own in the wild garden and I sense that I am losing part of myself as the boughs fall – though not very far, for they writhe in their Laocoon fashion only just above the grass. Once there was so much fruit I could hardly give it away, the locals not wanting 'the trouble'. All except my farmer neighbour William Brown who came to beg a few 'for my wife'. Welcome, welcome dear quince lover. John Nash, who may have planted the tree, liked to place a fat quince on the dashboard of his Triumph Herald, there to scent the car out. I made quince cheese, or put a bit of the fruit in an apple pie 'to quicken it'. Alas, wonderful *Cydonia oblonga*, how you have come down in the world! Once you scented the temples of Venus. A quarter of you is in late leaf so, rid of death, and with my having let the light in, pull yourself together and bring forth in abundance your hard-as-wood, yet delicate, yellow fruit just like you used to. For there remain a few of us who will take the trouble to make of you 'a precious Conserve and Marmalade, beeying congealed with long seethyng, and boiled with Sugar, Wine and Spices'. It is now as dark as midnight and the tools are swallowed up, enveloped, lost, and an owl cries imperiously. I feel my way home. On a shelf of cookbooks going back to the year dot I discover one published in Calcutta in 1919. Quinces, quinces, the yellowing pages turn. 'Quince cheese – press into tins lined with brandy papers'? 'It will take hours.'

A monthly Evensong for just half a dozen of us – more when it is light – but 'here two or three are gathered together in my Name', etc. And anyway it is a favourite service, sung without an organist, spoken with alternative voices, the candles wavering, the nave roof somehow floating and indistinct, barely above us, the Advent prayers. It is all so perfect, so beautiful, so 'enough'. But of course it won't save the world. What will?

The bellringers' dinner looms into the calendar and we crowd into the Crown, wear paper hats and devour turkey. We spy strangers from towers near and far, captains and masters who make the valley tumultuous when they have a mind to. Our bells reach from the Wars of the Roses to World War Two, and our Attempts reach dizzy numbers, as our pealboards boast. Some of us are ringers, churchwardens and organists all in one. You get your money's worth in the Church of England. I think of my father standing in the dark garden when there was ringing practice, just to listen, just to soak the sound in. The noise in the pub is less listenable to, though there is no choice. Fifty eating ringers and their guests make a fine roar.

The Divine Adventure

December 7th

The friend and I agreed that the late autumn tidying of the wilder parts of our ramshackle farmhouse gardens is urgent. Dog-walkers wave from a distance and shout, 'We can see where you have been!' Fallen boughs are stacked for the stove, matted grass is combed out, shrubs are given a short back and sides, brambles are forked about. Meanwhile the pallid sun scoots behind black clouds. A thousand rooks appear like a sky river and all too soon evening tugs down the blinds, and I feel my way back to tea. Meanwhile, still safely imprisoned in my diary are all the Christmas services, more than ever every year. And free as air comes Advent – God's adventure in becoming one of us. We call him every lovely name which comes into our heads: Emmanuel, Wisdom from on High, Desire of Nations, Dayspring, Lord of David's Key! Welcome, welcome child, unwelcome Judge. How old-fashioned judgement sounds. People once quaked at the very mention of it. We see before us the boy in his mother's arms, not the great assize. Not the 'awful pomp, and earth aghast' but a rural birthday.

I remember my old friend Denis Garrett telling me about his famous cousin Elizabeth Garrett Anderson, the first woman mayor as well as doctor, who to the horror of the alderman gave up living in the big house after the death of her husband for a flat in the stable. This about 1912, and at Aldeburgh. The indignity of it! So they arrived to make her see sense, they in awful pomp, she aghast. She heard them out then turned them out – 'Why, your Maker was *born* in a stable!'

The Collects for Advent, especially the first one, are simply magnificent. And the last epistle says simply, 'The Lord is at hand. Be careful for nothing . . . and the peace of God, which passeth all understanding, shall keep your hearts

and minds through Jesus Christ.' We should sing Eleanor
Farjeon's 'People, look East', but we won't.

> Furrows, be glad. Though earth is bare,
> One more seed is planted there:
> Give up your strength the seed to nourish,
> That in course the flower may flourish.
> People, look East, and sing to-day:
> Love the Rose is on the way.

I am writing the names of the people in the photographs,
listening to the radio and going through album by album
because, as they say, 'Who will know them when you have
gone?' Good question. The people are black and white and
sometimes coloured. The same person is all ages, young and
handsome, old and not so bad. The Nazis were doing their
worst when that shadow fell across our garden. Writers and
painters look up from their unremitting toil to grin. Aunts
smile in their best. Cats appear from nowhere, for who can
now tell where they came from, cats who dined on lights
and skimmed milk, smart cats who lived on mice and bits
from our table, and, latest of the line, the white cat who
eats nothing but the best. They look up at the camera when
they feel like it and are immortalized. What a job it is, this
naming of likenesses, this brave seeing myself at all ages in
and out of the house, in and out of the sea, R. B. 19 –.
The dead take such lively steps out of the dark-room. Will
posterity thank me?

When in Doubt

December 21st

I archaeologize the shorn track before the postman's tyres and my regular feet have smoothed its roughnesses. I have found flint arrows and loom-weights in my time. How harsh it looks, like the scraped heads one flinches from in the streets. I snip off waving blackberry fronds to stop them from giving the organist's car a loving scratch, and walk warily by the wild-bee bank just in case these furious creatures, already cross with Mr Sycamore and his track-subduing machine, might take it out on me. Gilbert White was equally cautious when he found nests of them near Lewes in September 1792: 'On the very summit of this exalted promontory (Mount Carburn), and amidst the trenches of its Danish Camp, there haunts a species of wild bee, making its nest in the chalky soil . . . which dash and strike around the heads and faces of intruders.' Mine, though wrathful, do not attack me but simply rush against their dusty palace in a buzz of displeasure. Above them waves Mr Bradshaw's dead-level wheat. Great and small flints, many with razor-sharp edges from having been split during ploughing, lie exposed. Can this one be an artefact? What is certain is they have all been touched by human hands, women's and children's hands for the most part, those tender stone-pickers of the past who made the village roads.

We light all four candles for St Thomas, the apostle of doubt. It is Evensong and we sing 'Disposer supreme' who entrusts his riches to 'frail earthen vessels, and things of no worth', and I remember the delicate hands which carried flints from the fields to cart-tracks for centuries. I also remember a worrying gravestone which said – this when I was a boy – 'There lives more faith in honest doubt, believe me, than in half the creeds.' It comes from Tennyson's *In Memoriam*, the lament for his young friend Arthur Hallam. St Thomas walked with Jesus towards the resurrection of Lazarus but was not able to believe in that Resurrection which took place soon after. He needed proof, and when it was given him he cried, 'My Lord and my God', words which were to be the first clear statement of the divinity of Christ. The allowance for doubt at the very beginning of the Church was a theological master-stroke, for it admitted our humanity. Let it in. Doubt is the disturbed thought which can settle faith. It was on the eve of St Thomas that poor Thomas More wrote to his daughter Margaret from the Tower,

> Our Lord bless you, good daughter, and your good husband, and your little boy, and all yours, and all my children, and all my godchildren and all our friends. I cumber you, good Margaret, much, but I would be sorry if it should be any longer than tomorrow, for it is St Thomas's eve; and therefore, tomorrow long I to go to God. It were a day very meet and convenient for me . . .

The Gospel for St Thomas's Evensong, 1 Peter 1, is reproachful. It speaks of the trial of faith of a Christ whom, though not seen, is loved. Which is the Christ of all of us. Behind me in the chancel glows the O'Connor window with the two sisters who had seen the resurrection of their brother, Mary listening, Martha staggering from the kitchen with a pile of plates. Sharp tongued they were about that late delivery from the tomb, and realistic, telling their dawdling Saviour what a state the corpse would now be in, and doubting if anything now could be done. What lives did those resurrected young folk lead? Not the lives they had lived before. Sensation could have dogged them, though not honest doubt.

Other People's Christmas

December 25th

The diarists and letter-writers squeeze against each other on the top shelves otherwise where would I be? Glued to their confessions and not working a minute. But happening to check on one of their Christmases, I cannot stop. Here is John Wesley.

> At the Love-feast which we had in the evening at Bristol, seventy or eighty of our brethren and sisters from Kingswood were present, notwithstanding the

heavy snow. We all walked back together, through the most violent storm of sleet and snow which I ever remember; the snow also lying above the knee deep in many places; but our hearts were warmed, so that we went on rejoicing and praising God for the consolation.

Here is Parson Woodforde in 1777.

Dec. 25. I went to Weston Church this morning at ½ past 10 and read Prayers and administered the H. Sacrament there, being Christmas Day. About 24 Communicants . . . Being Christmas Day the following poor people dined at my House, old Rich: Bates, old Rich: Buck, Thos Carr, old Thos Dicker, old Tom Cushion, Robin Buck and my clerk Js Smith . . . I had for dinner a fine surloin of Beef roasted and Plumb puddings for them.

John having made guards for our pew heaters, I remembered Colette at school:

Sometimes a baby pupil, who had tried to warm herself by sitting on her footwarmer, would let out a squeal, because she had burnt her little bottom. Or an odour would spread in the room from a chestnut, a potato, or a winter pear that one of us was trying to cook in her footwarmer . . . Surrounding us was the winter, a silence disturbed by crows, the moaning of the wind, the clatter of wooden shoes, winter, and the belt of woods encircling the village . . . Nothing else. Nothing more.

Daphne du Maurier, old now, finds herself at Menabilly alone:

> It's so queer having no one down here for Christmas. I have not done my routine decorating, but have put all my cards around, and have lovely flowers everywhere, and an arrangement of holly on the centre table in the Long Room, and so it all looks very cheerful. If I thought about it too deeply, I might be rather sad, but I don't ... I think the thing is always to look ahead in life, and never look back, except in gratitude ...

Francis Kilvert, the young curate of Clyro in 1870:

> Sunday, Christmas Day. As I lay awake praying in the early morning I thought I heard the sound of distant bells. It was an intense frost. I sat down in my bath upon a sheet of thick ice which broke in the middle into large pieces whilst sharp points and jagged edges stuck all around the sides of the tub like cheveux de frise, not particularly comforting to the naked thighs and loins ... I had to collect the floating pieces of ice and pile them on a chair before I could use the sponge ... The morning was most brilliant. Walked to the Sunday School with Gibbins and the road sparkled with a million rainbows ... The church was very cold in spite of two roaring stove fires. Mr Venables preached.

Katherine Mansfield is malcontented in Hampstead a month after the Armistice.

I wish we were all in France with a real Xmas party in prospect – snow, huge fire, a feast, wine, old old French tunes on a guitar, fancy dresses, a Tree, and everybody too happy for words. Instead we are wondering to give the postman 5 shillings . . . or 3 . . . This cursed country would take the spirit out of a Brandied Cherry.

On Christmas Day 1844 Cornelius Stoven, a Lincolnshire farmer, walks to the Methodist chapel at Binbrook.

When I reached the brow of the hill my ears were regailed by the sound of a band of music. Though the air was thick the clouds formed a good sounding board to carry and diffuse the Binbrook harmonies far and wide . . . The air was keen and frosty enough to stiffen my beard with rhyme [rime]. I enjoyed the prayer meeting and had the additional pleasure of reading Talmage's sermon on Amos's basket of summer fruit.

The nineteen-year-old Queen Victoria confided to her diary at Christmas-time that Lord Melbourne 'said that he thought almost everybody's character was formed by their Mother, and that if the children did not turn out well, the mothers should be punished for it. Lord Melbourne is very absent in company often, and talks to himself now and then, loud enough to be heard but never loud enough to be understood.'

On Christmas Eve 1974 Stephen Spender was in Jerusalem:

After dinner, to the Church of the Nativity, for Midnight Mass. The Church is large and bare, the Mass was intoned in Latin, with some dignity . . . The most beautiful part of the evening was after we left the service and walked back along the road the two miles to Rebecca's Well, where our car was parked. We heard, from that distance across the valley dividing us from Bethlehem, the voices from the Church still singing, which the cold night air seemed to purify of raggedness and wrong notes, so that coming from the hill above us, they seemed those of a heavenly choir.

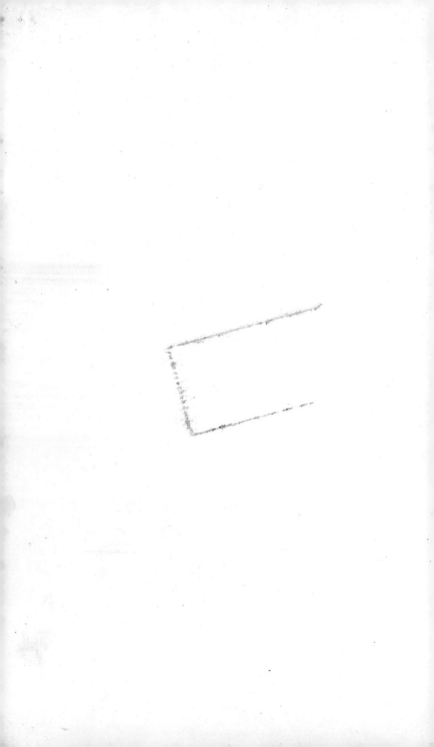